A Pocket Guide to College Success

A Pocket Guide to College Success

Jamie H. Shushan

The Crimson Summer Academy
at Harvard University

Bedford/St. Martin's   Boston ◆ New York

For Bedford/St. Martin's

*Publisher for College Success
    and Developmental Studies:* Edwin Hill
Senior Executive Editor for College Success: Simon Glick
Senior Development Editor: Christina Lembo
Developmental Editor: Julie Kelly
Senior Production Editor: Anne Noonan
Senior Production Supervisor: Lisa McDowell
Senior Marketing Manager: Christina Shea
Editorial Assistant: Bethany Gordon
Copy Editor: Linda McLatchie
Indexer: Melanie Belkin
Photo Researcher: Jennifer Atkins
Senior Art Director: Anna Palchik
Text Design: Claire Seng-Niemoeller
Cover Design: Billy Boardman
Composition: Graphic World Ltd.
Printing and Binding: RR Donnelley and Sons

President, Bedford/St. Martin's: Denise B. Wydra
Editorial Director for English and Music: Karen S. Henry
Director of Marketing: Karen R. Soeltz
Production Director: Susan W. Brown
Director of Rights and Permissions: Hilary Newman

Printed in China

8   7   6
f   e

For information, write: Bedford/St. Martin's, 75 Arlington Street, Boston, MA 02116   (617-399-4000)

ISBN 978-1-4576-1981-6

Acknowledgments

How to Use This Book

Stepping onto campus that first day isn't easy. But fortunately, you're not alone. You'll soon meet advisors, instructors, students, and many others supporting you throughout your college experience.

We want you to have the tools you'll need to succeed, which is why we've created this guide. It's filled with tips, strategies, and advice to help you get ahead in college. We're certain the advice offered within will help make the transition easier, your academic life more manageable and interesting, and your overall college experience more fulfilling.

This is a resource for YOU. As a college student, you're in the driver's seat and are expected to take advantage of the resources available on campus, to try new techniques to help you succeed in your classes, and to ask for assistance when you need it. You will reach your goals, as you always have, with perseverance, resilience, hard work, *and* the help of others.

Your fan,

Jamie H. Shushan

Jamie H. Shushan

Finding What You Need

A Pocket Guide to College Success is designed to provide clear answers to your questions about what to do, where to go, and how to succeed in college. It can help you in your first year, throughout your whole college career, and—hopefully—in your life beyond college. In this book, you will find the tools you need to survive and thrive as you begin this new journey.

Chapter 1 will help you build a college support system early on so you can ask the right questions and get the help you need. Chapters 2 through 4 discuss time management, learning styles, and critical thinking—key building blocks to success. Chapters 5 through 9 focus on key study skills strategies, complete with detailed study tips and helpful examples. Chapter 10 will help you with academic planning and selecting a major. Chapters 11 through 14 will help you with aspects of college life beyond academics: stress management, making healthy choices, coping with difference, navigating the social scene, and managing money. Chapter 15 helps answer the question "What's Next?" by referring back to key content presented earlier in the book and expanding on the topic of career exploration. Finally, Appendices A and B address some key issues and needs facing students who live on and off campus. For more details on these chapters, please see the Preface on pages viii–xiv.

Table of Contents. Browsing through the brief table of contents inside the front cover will usually guide you to the information you need. If not, consult the more detailed table of contents included inside the back cover.

Index. If you can't locate what you need in either table of contents, consult the index at the back of the book, beginning on page 223. The index can be especially useful if you're looking for something specific and you know the term for it. For example, if you want help creating a to-do list, you could simply look under "to-do list" in the index and then go to the designated pages.

Lists of Features. On pages 237–41 (just before the end of the book), you'll find a quick guide to some of the most often consulted parts of this book: Checklists, Quick Tips, Visual Walkthroughs (illustrated explanations of key points), "5 Things" lists, and Case Studies.

Other Useful Tools

Living on Campus. Appendix A (pp. 209–14) contains tips and advice for students who live on campus, such as avoiding conflicts with roommates, building relationships with residential advisors, and taking advantage of on-campus opportunities.

Living off Campus. Appendix B (pp. 215–20) offers guidance for students who live off campus, such as establishing a workable home/work/life balance and how getting involved in campus activities can support your overall success in college.

Preface for Instructors

A *Pocket Guide to College Success* is a unique handbook for college students, organized as a "go to" resource that's easy to dig into whenever necessary. In contrast to longer, traditional texts, creating a *handy* college guide that students could refer to quickly and easily was always the driving force behind this book.

A Pocket Guide to College Success is just that—a friendly resource, succinct and understandable, filled with digestible advice and doable strategies, that students from various backgrounds can refer to periodically in a first-year college success course, throughout their college years, in the years beyond college, or even before they enter college life.

Yet despite its brevity, *A Pocket Guide to College Success* still covers virtually all of the topics and advice typically found in much longer texts, in a format that your students will read and at a price that they will *definitely* appreciate.

A Pocket Guide to College Success has been designed to work well in a wide range of programs and institutions: at two- and four-year schools, in traditional first-year-experience seminars and courses, as part of "Common Read" programs, as part of orientation programs—and, of course, for programs that find full-size texts overwhelming, prohibitively expensive, or simply too much.

For many students, the first term of college can feel like visiting a foreign country. Suddenly, they have to learn how to navigate new customs, unfamiliar policies, and possibly even a new language. These students, and many others besides, could use practical strategies and advice to navigate the unfamiliar terrain. Each chapter of *A Pocket Guide to College Success* is written with an eye toward students whose understanding and information about college life are limited.

- **Chapter 1** helps students build a college support system early on so that they are able to ask the right questions and get the help they will need.

- **Chapters 2 through 4** discuss time management, learning styles, and critical thinking, all topics fundamental to success in college.

- **Chapters 5 through 9** focus on key study skills strategies. Study tips are explained step-by-step, and examples demonstrate how to actually use the tips, making *A Pocket Guide to College Success* accessible and usable.

- **Chapter 10** addresses two very important topics for today's students: academic planning and selecting a major. This chapter also introduces the topic of careers, which is covered in more depth in Chapter 15.

- **Chapters 11 through 14** look beyond academics towards other aspects of college life: stress management, making healthy choices, coping with difference, navigating the social scene, and managing money. *A Pocket Guide to College Success* gives students a much-needed "heads-up" about a number of college realities and provides sound advice to help them wade through the many decisions and situations they will face, hopefully improving their health, happiness, and safety in the long run.

- **Chapter 15** answers the question "What's Next?" by referring back to key content presented earlier in the book and expanding on the topic of career exploration. This chapter addresses how students can succeed in terms and years still to come.

- **Appendix A** addresses the specific issues and needs of students who live on campus, and **Appendix B** addresses the same topics for those who live off campus.

Features

- **Inexpensive, pocket-sized, and spiral bound.** *A Pocket Guide to College Success*'s comprehensive yet streamlined coverage, small size, and affordable price make it ideal for a wide range of students and uses in and out of the classroom.

- **A useful reference designed to help students focus on key concepts.** The clean design, clear and accessible writing style, and helpful charts signpost the most important concepts and ideas. Reference features and appendices help students find what they need when they need it.

- **Helpful learning and study features in each chapter.**
  - **Visual Walkthroughs** show core concepts of college success in action and focus on important skills such as developing a study plan, marking up a textbook, and taking notes.
  - **Case studies** show students from diverse backgrounds applying the strategies introduced.
  - **Summary Checklists** reinforce key concepts and help students assess their own progress.
  - **Quick Tips boxes and "5 Things" lists** offer practical advice.

- **Fun cartoons throughout the text** help anxious, stressed-out students relax with a little humor!

Instructor Resources

For more information or to order or download the instructor resources, please visit the online catalog at **bedfordstmartins.com/collegesuccess**.

- **Instructor's Manual.** The Instructor's Manual includes chapter teaching suggestions, a list of each chapter's features and how to use them, lecture ideas and activities, general teaching tips, and more. Available online.

- ***French Fries Are Not Vegetables.*** This comprehensive instructional DVD features multiple resources for class and professional use.

- **Custom with Care program.** Bedford/St. Martin's Custom Publishing offers the highest-quality books and media, created in consultation with publishing professionals who are committed to the discipline. Make *A Pocket Guide to College Success* more closely fit your course and goals by integrating your own materials, including only the parts of the text you intend to use in your course, or both. Contact your local Bedford/St. Martin's sales representative for more information.

- **TradeUp.** Bring more value and choice to your students' first-year experience by packaging *A Pocket Guide to College Success* with one of a thousand titles from Macmillan publishers at a 50 percent discount from the regular price. Contact your local Bedford/St. Martin's sales representative for more information.

Student Resources

For more information on student resources, please visit the online catalog at **bedfordstmartins.com /collegesuccess**.

- **Free book companion site: bedfordstmartins.com /collegesuccess/resources.** You and your students want powerful online content that you can use anywhere, anytime. The companion site for *A Pocket Guide to College Success* gives you both, with free and open resources for you to use. These resources include:
  - **Downloadable podcasts** offer quick advice on note-taking, money management, time management and many more topics.
  - **"Where to Go for Help" library of links** directs students to further online resources for support and much more.
  - **Student Life videos** illustrate important concepts, skills, and situations that students will need to understand and master to become successful at college. Each video ends with questions to encourage further contemplation and discussion.

- *Bedford e-Book to Go for A Pocket Guide to College Success.* Now your students can get an e-Book version of *A Pocket Guide to College Success* at about half the price of the print book. To learn more about this low-cost alternative, go to **bedfordstmartins.com /collegesuccess/ebooktogo**.

- **Additional e-Book formats.** You can also find PDF versions of our books when you shop online at our publishing partners' sites: CourseSmart, Barnes & Noble NookStudy; Kno; CafeScribe; or Chegg. To learn more, visit **bedfordstmartins.com/ aboutebooks**.

- *VideoCentral: College Success* is a premiere collection of videos for the college success classroom. The site features the 30-minute documentary *French Fries Are Not Vegetables and Other College Lessons: A Documentary of the First Year of College*, which follows five students through the life-changing transition of the first year of college. Learn more at **bedford-stmartins.com/collegesuccess**. *VideoCentral* also includes access to the following:
  - 16 brief *Conversation Starters* that combine student and instructor interviews on the most important topics taught in first-year seminar courses.
  - 16 accompanying video glossary definitions with questions that bring these topics to life.

- **Bedford e-Portfolio.** The Bedford e-Portfolio makes it easy for students to showcase their coursework and share the story of their unique learning experience, whether for their class, for their job, or even for their friends. With straightforward, flexible assessment tools, the Bedford e-Portfolio lets instructors map rubrics and learning outcomes to student work, or just invite students to start their collections. It's a perfect fit for college success students, and can help them in *all* their courses across the curriculum. For more information, visit **bedfordstmartins.com/ eportfolio**.

- ***The Bedford/St. Martin's Planner*** includes everything that students need to plan and use their time effectively, with advice on preparing schedules and to-do lists, along with blank schedules and calendars (monthly and weekly) for planning. Integrated into the planner are tips and advice on fixing common grammar errors, taking notes, and succeeding on tests; an address book; and an annotated list of useful Web sites. The planner fits easily into a backpack or purse, so students can take it anywhere. You can package it with a Bedford/St. Martin's text or order the planner as a stand-alone.

- ***Bedford/St. Martin's Insider's Guides.*** These concise and student-friendly booklets on topics that are critical to college success are a perfect complement to your textbook and course. Bundle one with *any* Bedford/St. Martin's textbook at no additional cost. Insider's Guides cover topics including *Academic Planning; Beating Test Anxiety; Building Confidence; Career Services; College Ethics and Personal Responsibility; College Etiquette; Community College; Credit Cards; Getting Involved on Campus; Global Citizenship; Returning Veterans;* and *Time Management.* For more information on ordering one of these guides with the text, go to **bedfordstmartins.com/collegesuccess**.

- ***Journal Writing: A Beginning.*** Designed to give students an opportunity to use writing as a way to explore their thoughts and feelings, this writing journal includes a generous supply of inspirational quotes placed throughout the pages, tips for journaling, and suggested journal topics. You can package it with a Bedford/St. Martin's text or order the journal as a stand-alone.

Acknowledgments

I want to thank my colleagues at Bedford/St. Martin's—Co-President, Macmillan Higher Education Joan Feinberg; President Denise Wydra; Publisher Edwin Hill;

Senior Executive Editor Simon Glick; Senior Development Editor Christina Lembo; Senior Production Editor Anne Noonan; Senior Marketing Manager Christina Shea; and Editorial Assistant Bethany Gordon—for their important contributions, expertise, and hard work. I am especially grateful to my editor, Julie Kelly, for her vision, guidance, creativity, and dedication every step of the way.

I also extend my deepest appreciation to Maxine Rodburg, whose endless support and encouragement made this exciting journey possible. And sincere thanks to Clayton Spencer, Don Pfister, Nancy Sommers, Bill Wright-Swadel, and Bob Cohen for opening so many doors. To the remarkable CSA Graduates I have been so fortunate to teach—you inspired me to write this guide and I am eternally grateful. Finally, to my family—Carol Horr, Jim Horr, Brian Harr, and Stacy Harr, as well as my husband, David Shushan, and children, Kevin and Nathan—special thanks for believing in me.

Thanks to all the instructors who participated in reviews: Carrie Cokely, *Curry College*; Karen Costa, *Mount Wachusett Community College*; Marcy Graham, *Truman State University*; Judith Kaufman, *Fairleigh Dickinson University*; Joseph Kornoski, *Montgomery County Community College*; Joanna Kourtidis, *University of St. Francis*; Jodi Kuznia, *St. Cloud State University*; Linda D. Morgan, *University of Alaska–Anchorage*; Katherine O'Brien, *Kent State University at Stark*; Carl Olds, *University of Central Arkansas*; Cynthia Pascal, *The Art Institute of Washington*; Stacey Peterson, *University of North Dakota*; Heather Simpson, *Michigan Technological University*; John Sugg, *Wingate University*; James Uhlenkamp, *Graceland University*; Denise Wilkinson, *Virginia Wesleyan College*; Shane Williamson, *Lindenwood University*; Craig Zywicki, *Iowa State University*.

Finding Support
on Campus

You're never alone at college. Classmates jam large lecture halls, students and faculty pass each other regularly on campus, and herds wait in line for meals in the food court. But you may still feel pangs of loneliness, even with this hustle and bustle. You might even feel isolated or afraid, especially during your first year. These feelings are completely normal because everything is new. You're in unfamiliar territory, with new faces, new rules, and new experiences. Moreover, real friendships take a lot of effort, and you need to give yourself time to develop authentic relationships with your peers. But as soon as you begin college, it is important to make connections with faculty and staff on campus and to begin building a system of support that you'll need throughout your undergraduate experience. Here is some advice to get you going.

Advising 101

As a first-year college student, you will be assigned an academic advisor who will meet with you throughout the year. This advisor will help you choose classes, discuss other aspects of college life, and answer any questions you might have. At the beginning of the year and at various points during each term, your advisor will schedule meetings to check in and discuss important topics with you. This relationship is invaluable because your advisor is a trusted resource you can turn to whenever you need advice about college. As you progress through your first year, communicating honestly with your advisor on a regular basis will help you feel more connected and supported, especially if questions or difficulties arise.

Advisors Are Integral to Success

You should give a great deal of thought to your course selection, and your advisor is an important voice in this decision-making process. Talk with him or her about your interests and your future goals. Which fields of study do you want to explore during your first year to give you a better sense of what you might major in later on? What careers would you like to pursue after you graduate, or are you undecided? Your advisor will listen carefully and can help you navigate the course catalog, providing guidance as to which courses are most appropriate. Advisors are also aware of college requirements and will talk with you about whether you should take certain required courses during your first year. Picking the right course load based on your interests and college requirements is a team effort and will help you succeed in college.

Build a Relationship with Your Advisor

Your advisor is an academic resource, but you might want to share other aspects of college life with him or her. For example, advisors are also resources to help students navigate the transition from high school to college, manage roommate issues, and find a balance between courses and extracurricular activities. If you are working or caring for family members while attending classes, advisors can help you find a course load that is reasonable given the many responsibilities you're juggling. Don't hesitate to share what's on your mind with your advisor; if your advisor doesn't have the answer, it's his or her job to connect you to other resources on campus.

Share your history. An advisor can only be as effective as the information he or she has to work with. Sharing your academic history, including any past struggles you've had, will improve your advisor's ability to advise you. For example, if you have always suffered from test anxiety, your advisor can suggest appropriate academic resources to assist you.

Practice honest communication. You may be paired with an outstanding advisor who's always available, interested in getting to know you, and willing to talk about everything from class selection to roommate issues. But what if you find it difficult to talk to your advisor? Maybe you feel intimidated, or maybe the two of you struggle to communicate effectively. If so, be honest with yourself and your advisor about the difficulty you're having. This type of honesty often opens up lines of communication, especially if your advisor isn't aware of the problem.

If you can't improve your relationship with your advisor, visit the Advising Office and explain what's going on. Request another advisor; if that's not possible, set up a meeting with someone else in the Advising Office who can answer your questions. Advocating for your needs in this way will help you in the long run.

Create a College Network

Creating a college network is crucial. The more faculty and staff you meet early on in your college career, the more support you're building for yourself and the more likely it is that you'll find a few people to whom you feel particularly connected and whom you can trust. These become your mentors. When you have others on campus who know you well, they will be able to give you advice.

Mentors are invaluable resources. A mentor might be an instructor you have worked with closely in the classroom, a coach you see regularly, or a college staff member you interact with frequently. During your first year, try to get to know at least one person on campus well enough to consider him or her your mentor. This relationship is invaluable because mentors are invested in your well-being and want to offer assistance when they can.

Nourish mentoring relationships regularly. Keep your mentor updated on how you're doing throughout college. Seek out your mentor when you need advice or support or when you just want to share an exciting life development. The more you develop this relationship, the more your mentor can serve as an advocate and a wise counsel as you deal with the regular ups and downs of college.

⑤ WAYS TO MAKE THE MOST OF YOUR MENTOR RELATIONSHIP

1. **Schedule lunch dates or meetings every two to three months.**

   Getting together on a regular basis will enable you to stay connected and will make it easier to reach out for help when you need to.

2. **Talk about your future goals, not just what's happening in your life right now.**

   Sharing your goals will help your mentor better understand who you are, where you want to go, and how he or she can be most helpful along the way.

3. **Ask about your mentor's life to learn from his or her experiences.**

   Meaningful relationships happen when there is mutual understanding, so while you're talking about your life, be sure to ask about your mentor's life. You might be surprised what you learn.

4. **Share not only your achievements but also any difficulties you are experiencing.**

   Don't be afraid to share what isn't going well for you. Your mentor is a resource you should be able to trust with any struggles you encounter.

5. **Thank your mentor when his or her advice and support have proved helpful.**

   A simple thank-you, whether written or offered in person, is an important gesture, especially since your mentor may not know the impact he or she has made.

Important Offices to Visit

In addition to advisors and mentors, a number of offices on college campuses also provide valuable support. Many of these student resources are described below (the names of these offices will vary by institution). During your first term, try to learn what types of resources your college offers. You might want to schedule a meeting

No matter how large or complex your campus is, it takes time to figure out how to find all the resources at your college. Give yourself that time, be patient, and reach out to the many campus supports available to you.

with a staff member in these offices so that you will be more comfortable seeking advice whenever you need it.

Additional Academic Advising Resources

Your advisor isn't the only person at your college who is able to provide advice. Other resources on campus can help you if you're looking for a second opinion on course selection or if you're struggling to get the answers you need from your assigned advisor. The following resources can offer you additional academic advising.

Academic Advising Office. Find the Academic Advising Office (or equivalent office) at your college and schedule a meeting with a staff member who can answer your questions.

First-Year Programs Office. Staff members in the First-Year Programs Office are focused solely on the experience of first-year students, so stop by and find out if an advisor can assist you.

Specific academic departments. If you have questions about specific classes and major requirements, meet with a departmental advisor in a particular field of study (for example, biology, psychology, or English).

Try one, two, or all three of these resources because the more perspectives you get, the better informed you'll be, as Lisa's experience demonstrates.

 CASE STUDY

Lisa, in her first term of college, dealt with a challenging advising situation. But after advocating for herself, she managed to turn the situation around. Here is her story.

My assigned advisor was not very helpful. When I tried reaching him for academic advice, he was never available. He wasn't very personable, and that intimidated me. I didn't get the support I needed, and the lack of support discouraged me from seeking more help. I talked with a few upperclassmen I trusted, who suggested that I visit the First-Year Programs Office. I finally decided that things weren't going to change unless I took some initiative, so after class one day I stopped by the First-Year Programs Office. An advisor in the office took the time to meet with me, and we hit it off. I asked her if she could be my new advisor, and she happily agreed. I had to let my old advisor know. The encounter was slightly awkward, but ultimately he seemed fine with my decision. My new advisor was welcoming, encouraging, and realistic, qualities I needed as an insecure first-year student. When I had questions, she would direct me to the right person or would try to point me in the right direction. She was my advisor until I declared my major and found an advisor in the International Relations Department. However, she remained an unofficial advisor and mentor, and I continued to meet with her often.

QUESTIONS FOR REFLECTION: Does Lisa's story resonate with your advising experience? Have you received the advising that you need to feel supported? Do you know of any other advising resources you should tap into?

Other Supportive Resources

Colleges are aware that students will experience much exciting growth while they pursue their degrees; for this reason, colleges provide many resources dedicated to supporting students in both their academic and personal lives. Colleges also offer services to assist with financial matters and to help with job and career questions.

Academic Support and Tutoring Office.   You may find yourself struggling in a class. Instead of relying on your classmates to help you, check out the services at your college's Academic Support and Tutoring Office. Whether you're having difficulty with the reading load, experiencing trouble studying and remembering information, or receiving low grades on quizzes and tests, take advantage of all that the college offers, including tutoring. Colleges can usually find tutors in any subject area or at the very least will determine what resources are available to help you.

Writing and math centers.   Your college campus might have other key academic resources, such as a writing center and a math center. Determine what these centers offer and when they're open. Use the writing center if you need help with an assigned paper—even if you think it's well written—or if you are struggling with written exams. Use the math center to help you complete homework assignments, understand important concepts, or finish tests in the time allotted. Each of these centers offers one-on-one help and serves as a place to study so that you have immediate access to assistance if you run into difficulty.

Counseling centers. Campuses have various counseling offices dedicated to supporting students with any challenges they might face during college, including academic struggles, personal issues, and social dilemmas. You might seek assistance from a counselor if you're experiencing test anxiety, constantly feel overwhelmed, have medical problems, or are dealing with roommate or family difficulties. During college, it's normal to experience tough times that require more than friendly advice from a peer. College counselors understand students' struggles and can offer needed support.

Financial Aid Office. During your first few weeks on campus, introduce yourself to your financial aid officer. Financial issues or questions can arise at any time, so having a connection in the Financial Aid Office is a great advantage. The conversations you have with him or her will demystify the financial aid process, making it easier when you apply for financial aid throughout your college years.

Career Services Office. The sooner you find your way to the Career Services Office, the sooner you'll discover the many resources this office provides, including career advice, assistance with summer jobs, and counseling to help you determine which classes and majors are appropriate for you.

Student Services Center. To learn how to get involved in campus activities, visit the Student Services Center (or equivalent office), where you can meet with staff who oversee campus activities and clubs. Determine how you'd like to connect with your peers through your college's various options. Building a connection to campus beyond the classroom will help you feel supported and more at home.

The library. Not only does the library offer books, journals, and online resources, but it also provides many supportive services for students. Librarians have research expertise that you can draw on, and they will help you find the information you need for assignments. Also available are computer and printing services.

Disability Services Office. If you need disability services of any kind, be sure to seek support from your campus Disability Services Office. Staff members will determine how best to assist you.

Diversity centers. Campus diversity centers provide a space for students of different ethnic, religious, or cultural backgrounds to come together in a variety of ways. You will find opportunities to organize multicultural events, join clubs, participate in discussions, meet with center staff members, or enjoy a place to study and socialize.

The offices described above are staffed with people who want to support students through the college experience. Use these valuable resources whenever and as often as you need them.

✅ CAMPUS RESOURCES CHECKLIST

Locate and visit the following campus resources on campus or online:

- ☐ Academic Support and Tutoring Office
- ☐ Counseling Center
- ☐ Financial Aid Office
- ☐ Career Services Office
- ☐ Student Services Center
- ☐ Library
- ☐ Disability Services Office
- ☐ Diversity Center

Instructors Have Offices Too

When considering the many student support offices on campus, don't forget the support you'll receive by visiting your instructors in their offices. Don't rely on e-mail as your only means of communication. Take the time to talk with your instructors so that they understand who you are as a student, beyond your test scores and paper grades. Show your instructors your interest in the courses they teach, and ask them thoughtful questions so that they can see the effort you're putting into studying the course material. Spend time getting their advice about papers and studying, and discuss aspects of the course that you don't understand. Getting to know your instructors can help you in your college career, especially if you are struggling in some way.

Make the Most of Office Hours

The first week of class, instructors usually post their office hours—the hours during the week when they are available to meet with students. Visiting an instructor during office hours is a great way to meet privately with him or her to introduce yourself, discuss interesting aspects of the class, share your progress on a paper, talk about your grade on the last quiz, or ask for studying and

QUICK TIP

Be Prepared

Before you visit an instructor during office hours, spend five to ten minutes preparing for the meeting. Write down the questions you'd like to ask, and flag any material you don't understand or want to discuss. If you need advice on a paper, brainstorm your ideas for a paper topic before you meet with your instructor. If you want some help with a problem set, make an honest effort to work on the problem set beforehand so that your instructor knows you tried your best.

Find Campus Resources Online

During the first few weeks on campus, take time to explore the various links on your college's Web site. Campus resources—such as academic support, counseling services, financial aid, and career services—usually have their own pages. And the college's Web site often lists club and athletic-related information, on-campus events, transportation schedules, and town/city happenings.

Current Students

Make the most of your UMass Amherst education by embracing all of the opportunities, resources, and the diversity of our campus. Take advantage of the broad range of academic programs and the Five College Interchange. Consider co-curricular options, internships and co-ops, and study abroad to lay the foundation for a rewarding career. Rely on our network of campus support services to provide key assistance as you work steadily toward your goals.

Academic Resources

- Academic Advising
- Community Service Learning
- Five College Interchange
- General Education Program (Gen Ed)
- Graduate Programs and Degrees
- Graduate Student Handbook
- Graduation Information
- Learning Commons
- Libraries
- Office of Undergraduate Research and Studies
- Registrar
- Study Abroad
- Tutoring and Supplemental Instruction

Financial Services

- Bursar's Office (Bill Payment)
- Financial Aid Services
- Graduate Assistantships
- Scholarships
- Student Employment

Daily Life

- Bookstore
- Bus Schedules and Maps
- Campus Recreation and Sport Clubs
- Center for Student Development
- Dean of Students
- Dining on Campus
- Family Housing
- Fraternities and Sororities
- Health Services
- Personal Safety
- Registered Student Organizations
- Residential and Spiritual Life
- Student Government Association
- Student Success Centers

Services and Resources

- Career Services
- Counseling and Psychological Health
- Diversity Matters
- Everywoman's Center
- Graduate Employee Organization
- Multicultural Programs and Services

1. Use this academic support office for one-on-one help whenever you are experiencing academic challenges in your courses.

2. Find answers to financial aid questions, meet with officers when you have concerns, learn more about your aid package, and access forms you need to fill out each year.

3. Check out this page if you're interested in participating in campus sports or recreational activities and want to learn about ways to stay healthy and fit.

4. Visit for advice and information about careers, summer internships, résumé writing, job applications, and more; take advantage of counseling services to help determine what classes and majors are appropriate for you.

5. Learn about the many opportunities to meet and find support from students and staff from diverse backgrounds, including mentoring, social events, clubs and organizations, cultural enrichment, and academic assistance.

Identify the Problem

Take time to figure out why you are having difficulty in a class. Are you studying a subject completely new to you? Did you struggle with similar material in high school? Do you have test-taking anxiety? Do you lack the needed study skills? Are you having difficulty writing papers in the style expected? By stepping back and assessing the root of your academic challenges, you can understand why you're having trouble. Be sure to share this information with your instructor so that he or she can offer more targeted assistance.

---

test-taking advice. Talking privately with your instructor might feel a bit daunting, but these meetings can make a big difference in helping you understand the material and improving your ultimate performance in the course.

Share Your Academic Struggles

The academic rigor of college courses usually surpasses that of high school courses. Therefore, most students face real challenges in college-level classes. And until you become familiar with college ways of studying, taking tests, and writing papers, you might not earn the grades you did in high school. If you find yourself struggling with course material at any point during the term, meet with your instructors after class or during office hours. They will see your effort and your desire to succeed, even if your grades don't seem to match, and they will help you in whatever ways they can.

Ask Questions and Get Help Often

Even after working with your advisor, meeting with staff in an academic support center, and visiting your instructor during office hours, you might still feel uncertain, overwhelmed, and alone. Even though you may think that everyone else knows what to do, where to go, what classes to pick, how to study, and what extracurricular activities to join, many students hide their real fears, academic struggles, and confusion in order to look good around their peers. In fact, most students, especially during their first year, experience anxiety, but few are willing to be honest about it.

Anxiety Is Understandable

Walking into a college world that is different from what you are used to can be scary, especially because everything is new to you. You need to pick classes, often without knowing what you will major in, and you're constantly faced with important decisions: Is this activity worth my time? What requirements should I fulfill this term? How many hours a week should I be studying and working? Dealing with all the newness and decision making can be very jarring, especially because you may feel as though you're the only one who doesn't fit in. However, it's perfectly normal if you find it challenging to manage certain aspects of your new college life. Fortunately, you don't have to manage them alone.

Seeking Assistance Is Key

Reach out to the college's many resources if you need help for any reason—academic or personal. Too many college students pretend that they don't need help with their course work, when in fact they are struggling. Or they try to dismiss difficult personal or social pressures that continue to build. These students are fooling themselves and will only suffer as a result. Acknowledging that college may be challenging for you is the first step toward facing your fears and persevering. Success in college requires the courage to ask questions all the time and to get help as soon as you need it.

College supports. Remember your many college supports. Talk to your advisor, have lunch with a mentor, meet with an instructor, go to an academic center, work with a tutor, or make an appointment with a counselor.

Be an advocate for yourself by reaching out to those who want to help you.

Peer supports. Don't underestimate the level of support you may receive from fellow classmates and upperclassmen. Being honest with peers can increase levels of trust and build a deeper connection with them. Building connections with your classmates will improve your sense of belongingness on campus because you have spoken honestly about your feelings, allowing others to share openly as well.

Family and friends. Reaching out to family members and friends can also provide a level of support that is integral to feeling secure on campus because it creates an important connection between your personal life and your new academic life.

Getting help in college is a courageous act. It's also an essential life skill. In any job or relationship, being able to ask questions and reach out for help leads to successful careers and fulfilling lives. We all experience fear and struggles, but being able to find the right support helps get us through difficult times.

Managing your time effectively in college is the most important skill you can master, but it's also one of the most difficult. *Time management* may sound like a simple concept, but some students don't take it seriously, causing stress and academic problems. If you practice the following three suggestions, you'll be on the right track:

- Keep your daily and academic schedule in one place.
- Write down *everything*.
- Save time by planning and then prioritizing.

Remember: you're in the driver's seat in college. No one is forcing you out of bed in the morning, making you go to class, or checking whether you've started your assignments. And each day is slightly different. You might have three classes on Monday and Wednesday, one on Tuesday, lab on Thursday, and no classes on Friday. Additionally, college work isn't structured like it was in high school. You have to do most of it outside of class. You're in charge of your time, and it's up to you to make the most of each moment.

Time Is of the Essence

The amount of unstructured time in college is empowering, but it is also a big responsibility. How much should you study? When should you start assignments? How many hours should you devote to reading, writing papers, and labs? And how do you fit all this in without neglecting your other responsibilities—work, family commitments, extracurricular activities, and hopefully some fun?

Given all the activities you have to juggle, you literally have to *spend* time *managing* your time, which will ultimately *save* you time. Within the first term of college, you should try to master certain strategies for effective time management. These time management skills will serve you well throughout your college years and will also be invaluable when you enter the working world.

© Mike Baldwin / Cornered

"'Principles of Time Management'
was due back six months ago."

▲

*Don't fret if you experience some difficulty in managing your
time in college. Time management is a skill that you can master.
Make it a priority to practice some of the time management tips
in this chapter to figure out what works for you.*

Use a Planner

Maybe you have already used a planner, or maybe you
didn't need one because your friends had similar
schedules or your family members kept you on track.
Whatever the case, trying to juggle the many responsibilities of college in your head is a tough job, so using a
planner will be invaluable.

Planning will relieve stress. Using a planner leaves less
room for error. You are more likely to remember
assignment due dates and know when tests are approach-
ing. Staying organized in this way helps you gain control

of your daily life, reducing stress as you manage your college responsibilities.

Keeping track. Juggling academics, social life, work, and extracurricular activities isn't easy. But if you plan out each day, you will know how these pieces of your college life fit together. Becoming an expert in organizing your college life takes practice.

With more planning comes more time. It may seem counterintuitive, but the more time you take to plan, the more free time you'll have. In college, you will have a lot of unstructured time. Although you might view non-class time as free time, you'll have to spend much of that unstructured time completing assignments, studying for tests, and fulfilling job and extracurricular responsibilities. In general, you should expect to spend about 2 to 3 hours studying (ie. completing assignments and preparing for tests) outside of class, for every credit hour you spend in class. If you take 15 credit hours of class per week, you'll probably end up spending 30 to 45 hours per week studying outside of class. Only when you clearly lay out these academic commitments and other responsibilities will your actual free time become apparent.

QUICK TIP

Relax and Recharge
Use your free time to rejuvenate yourself. Take time to relax and care for your health. Recharging your battery frequently will make it easier for you to successfully juggle your college life.

Choose Your Planner Wisely

You can choose from many types of planners, including Web-based organizers such as Google Calendar. Some people prefer paper calendars or bound planners. Other people prefer the planner capabilities on smartphones and iPads. Whatever you choose, it's helpful to figure out a system that keeps all aspects of your college life in one place.

Schedule details of your daily life. It's important to write down everything you need to do each day in your planner:

- Academic life, including class times, labs, instructors' office hours, advising meetings, study sessions, and tutoring appointments
- Work responsibilities
- Extracurricular activities, including club meetings, sports practices, and games
- Personal life, including social gatherings, family commitments, and entertainment

---

QUICK TIP

Make Yourself a Priority

Add mealtimes, exercise plans, and sleep goals to your planner. Doing so can help motivate you to take better care of yourself. For example, if you work much better after a power nap, add a time slot for a nap to your planner so that it becomes a priority.

Add assignment and test details. Most instructors will distribute a syllabus on the first day of class. A syllabus is a road map of the class. In it, the instructor lists all assignment and reading due dates, test information, office hours, and anything else relevant to the class. Add this information to your planner for each course so that you have all the essential class details in one place.

Make a study plan. Developing a study plan is one of the most important study strategies you should master. Writing down *what day* you will begin assignments and *what day* you will start studying for tests can greatly improve your chances for college success. This aspect of time management—mapping out an assignment and study plan—can mean the difference between quality work and rushed work, or between an all-nighter of cramming for a test and a good night's sleep before taking the exam.

Map out your assignment and study plan during the first week of classes, after you have added all due dates and test dates to your planner.

> ✓ **TIME MANAGEMENT CHECKLIST**
>
> 1. Schedule the details of your daily life in your planner:
> - ☐ Academic life (classes, labs, office hours, advising meetings, tutoring)
> - ☐ Work life (job hours, staff meetings)
> - ☐ Extracurricular life (meetings, events, practices, games)
> - ☐ Personal life (social engagements, family commitments, TV)
> - ☐ Meals, exercise, and sleep
> 2. Add assignment due dates and test dates to your planner:
> - ☐ Readings
> - ☐ Papers and speeches
> - ☐ Projects
> - ☐ Labs and problem sets
> - ☐ Quizzes, tests, and exams
> 3. Map out your academic plan in your planner:
> - ☐ What day you'll begin each assignment
> - ☐ What day you'll start studying for each test

QUICK TIP

Sound the Alarm

Online calendars, such as Google Calendar, can be synched with your phone or other technology devices. That way you'll always have your calendar at your fingertips and can use built-in tools, such as alarm reminders, to help you remember when to go to class, what to prepare for class, when to complete assignments and study for tests, instructors' office hours, meeting times, sports practices, social events, and so on.

Battling Procrastination

So, your planner is now full of important information—
you've detailed your daily schedule, written down
important class dates in your planner, and mapped out
when you will start these assignments and begin
studying for tests. But what if you find yourself procrastinating when you have to start an assignment? A simple
but helpful time management tool is a daily prioritized
to-do list. Before going into more detail, let's take a
minute to consider why you might procrastinate.

Why Do You Procrastinate, and What Can You Do?

Procrastination is a powerful force that most of us deal
with daily. It can be especially powerful in college for a
number of reasons:

- The academic material you're studying is particularly
  challenging or confusing, so you would rather put it
  off or work on easier tasks first.

- You're not interested in the topics you're studying, so
  it's difficult to motivate yourself to get going.

- Other activities or tasks are more fun than your academic work, so it's easy to put off what you don't
  want to do.

- You're overwhelmed by the amount of work you have
  to do, and you don't know where to start.

- Distractions, often in the form of technology, occupy
  so much of your time that you end up avoiding the
  work that needs to be done.

This list is not exhaustive, but it might get you
thinking about why you procrastinate. In fact, when
you find yourself procrastinating, try to acknowledge
it. Being honest with yourself about procrastination
will actually help you combat it. You can then determine why you're procrastinating so that you can find
targeted strategies to overcome your procrastination,
such as those on the following page.

Tackle challenging assignments first. This strategy may seem counterintuitive, but if you work on difficult assignments first, they can feel less threatening and will become easier to accomplish. Moreover, because you're often more focused at the start of study sessions, you'll be at your best.

Build in rewards. In college, as in life, we sometimes have to do things that don't interest us. You can motivate yourself to get started on those types of tasks by rewarding yourself *after* you've completed them.

Include both academic and fun activities. All work and no play is not a recipe for success in college. Finding a balance that includes time for academics and time for fun will make you happier and more productive.

Break your work into chunks. You can make complex assignments and tests more manageable if you break them into smaller chunks. For instance, divide a ten-page paper into a series of smaller assignments that includes (1) developing a thesis, (2) outlining the paper, (3) writing the introductory paragraph, (4) writing pages one to five, and (5) writing pages five to ten.

Work in intervals and take breaks. Just as you break your work into manageable chunks, break your study sessions into forty-five-minute intervals, each followed by a ten-minute break.

Use a To-Do List

Everyone has a different method for creating a to-do list, but be sure to include everything that you hope to do in a day—both academic and personal. Academic items on your list might include writing the introduction to a paper, completing a class reading, or studying for a quiz. Nonacademic items might include running an errand, planning for a club fundraiser, spending time on Facebook, or watching your favorite television show.

Prioritize your list. Figuring out what needs to get done first, second, third, and so on can help you avoid procrastination. A list of prioritized tasks serves as a

⑤ WAYS SMART STUDENTS COMBAT PROCRASTINATION

1. **Schedule study dates with a classmate to keep each other on task.**

   Using your planner to set aside designated study times, especially with other students, will increase your motivation to complete work.

2. **Move to a different location when your room or home becomes too much of a distraction.**

   Your room or home may simply feel too comfortable. If you're distracted by the temptation of your bed, noisy roommates if you have any, or the desire to clean rather than do work, try moving somewhere else if it'll help you overcome procrastination.

3. **Set smartphone alarms to remind you to get working.**

   We love using our smartphones, so why not use them to tell you to get going on your work!

4. **Give friends permission to point out when you're procrastinating.**

   It can be annoying when others tell you to get working. But if you tell your friends that doing so will help motivate you, it just might do the trick, especially if they join you in hitting the books.

5. **Block out a few thirty-minute chunks to enjoy Facebook and respond to e-mail rather than checking periodically throughout the day.**

   Dedicating blocks of time for different tasks will increase your productivity and also can give you something to look forward to after you work on assignments.

road map. You know exactly where to start, and the list will propel you forward because you have a detailed plan in a particular sequence, without any ambiguity. You also might want to create a symbol system that indicates which items on your list are very important.

Determine what must get done. As you prioritize your list, indicate clearly what must get done that day and what could wait until the following day or later in the week. This step is important because the unexpected will happen and life circumstances may intervene, even if

Visual Walkthrough

Incorporate To-Do Lists into Your Planner

To get a good sense of what tomorrow will bring, put together your daily to-do list the night before. Then, in your planner, you can note when you'll try to complete each task. For example, after you write your to-do list on Sunday night, look at Monday's schedule and determine when you would like to tackle each item on the list.

TO-DO LIST	
FOR MONDAY	①
1. Econ. problem set (must finish—due tomorrow) ‼️	②
2. Study Sociology quiz (could wait—quiz Wed.)	
3. Write 3-4 pages of English paper (could wait—due Fri.)	
4. Attend Econ. office hours (ask about upcoming test) ???	

PLANNER	
MONDAY	
7–8 a.m.	
8–9 a.m.	BREAKFAST
9–10 a.m.	Math class
10–11 a.m.	Sociology class
11–12 p.m.	Economics professor office hours (Hall E, Rm. 301)
12–1 p.m.	LUNCH
1–2 p.m.	Work on Economics problem set (library)
2–3 p.m.	Start studying for Sociology quiz (library)
3–4 p.m.	Meet w/ advisor (Acad. Office, Rm. 101)
4–5 p.m.	Volunteer at Shelter (45 Carey St.)
5–6 p.m.	
6–7 p.m.	DINNER
7–8 p.m.	Gym
8–9 p.m.	Work on English paper (home)
9–10 p.m.	
10–11 p.m.	Study for Sociology quiz (home)
11–12 p.m.	SLEEP
12–6 a.m.	

1. Note what must get done and what could wait.

2. Symbols, such as exclamation points and question marks, can flag particularly important items on your list.

3. When you have unstructured time, write down what you'd like to work on during those hours. By telling yourself what time you'd like to complete an item on your to-do list, you will use your time more efficiently and you will know when you have true free time.

4. Indicate where you plan to work on your assignments and study for tests. These location details may affect your schedule if you have to build in travel time.

you have the best plan in place. You may not complete every task on your to-do list for a variety of reasons—an assignment took twice as long as you expected; an emergency came up; you got sick; or you forgot about a meeting you needed to attend.

Expect the Unexpected

If you need to, be ready to rework your to-do list and assignment schedule throughout the day. Move whatever didn't get done to another day so that you don't forget to complete these tasks. If you are flexible in updating your schedule, you will be prepared to deal with any unforeseen circumstances that may arise.

CASE STUDY

Mason describes his struggles with procrastination and how he has helped himself.

The times in college when I struggled with procrastination were when I failed to set clear time frames for when to work and when to socialize or do other activities. The hardest part about college is balancing the desire to hang out with friends with the need to complete the assignments due the next day. My strategy is to identify where I have the biggest chunk of time, taking into account any classes or meetings I might have during the day. This usually works for me because I tend to work most effectively when I have large periods of time.

My best advice for incoming college students is to start everything early. There is absolutely no reason to be stressed about deadlines or not having enough time to do work. Homework may not always be fun, but it doesn't have to feel like a chore. If you build homework into your daily schedule, it will feel like the next logical step in the progression of your day.

Something I wish I knew before entering college about time management is the benefit of keeping a physical agenda. I got great advice to do this, but being of this high-tech generation, I decided to keep an online agenda that ended up crashing on me, and I lost everything!

QUESTIONS FOR REFLECTION: When are you most likely to procrastinate? Does the time of day or type of work you're engaged in matter? What distractions are most difficult to ignore? Have you figured out strategies that help you overcome your procrastination tendencies? Are they working? If not, do you need help from an advisor, an instructor, or an academic support office?

Finding a Balance

When managing your time in college, you have to make difficult choices in order to find a balance that works for you. You are always faced with competing priorities, and although college is filled with a lot of unstructured time, instructors expect that you will devote most of this unstructured time to academic work. To strike a manageable balance, use your planner as a guide to determine what you can realistically fit in on any given day and in any given week.

Always Start with Academics

As you may have already discovered, the amount of work assigned in college is greater than what was assigned in high school. Readings and papers are longer, lab work is more complicated, problem sets are more involved, and tests are more challenging. Because of the volume of work in college, you must schedule time to work on academics every day, spreading out your assignments and studying over the course of the week and the weekend. Your instructors might not assign homework every day, but *you* must assign yourself homework each day using your planner and the time management strategies outlined in this chapter.

Your Schedule Will Lead the Way

By using a planner that allows you to see how much academic work you need to do each day and each week, you'll have a better sense of what else you can add to your life. Or you might realize that you need to cut back on extracurricular activities or even job hours, if that's possible. Organizing your time in a planner will help you make these important decisions.

In college, you need to make many decisions: How many hours can you realistically devote to your job? Should you consider becoming a leader in an on-campus organization, given the additional hours required for the position? When will you fit in exercise? Do you have time to add an extra class to your schedule, and if so, do you have enough hours left to complete assignments and study for tests? Your planner, which outlines your daily and weekly schedule, will be invaluable as you assess what you can and cannot handle.

All Work and No Play Isn't a Good Solution

Students do their best work when activities that bring joy and fulfillment are part of their daily routine. When you're assessing your daily and weekly schedule, be sure to carve out some time for fun, relaxation, physical activity, and a meaningful hobby or passion. Don't just work and sleep day after day. Look at your planner to determine how much time you have for enjoyable activities, and then find an activity that matches both your interests and how much time you can devote to it. For example, if you enjoy dance but have only two hours a week available, try to find a one-hour dance class that's offered twice a week.

Be Flexible

Your circumstances may change at any time during the term, so it's important to stay flexible when developing your schedule. Remember: the details in your planner are not set in stone. For example, you might need to change the amount of time you devote to a particular class if you find that the course work is more challenging or time-consuming than you expected. Similarly, you may need to adjust your schedule if you're struggling in a class and realize that you need regular tutoring sessions. If your involvement in an extracurricular activity intensifies, you might need to cut back on the number of hours you work.

Whatever the case, as you master the skill of time management, you'll be better able to find a balance that works for you—a balance that keeps you not only busy and productive but happy as well.

Chapter 3
Your Learning Style

Y ou may have noticed that you learn better depending on the way in which material is presented. Maybe you have a hard time remembering information that's presented verbally in a lecture, but if you're engaged in hands-on activities, you understand without a problem. Similarly, you may enjoy being assigned group projects because vocalizing what you've learned with peers pushes you to think in new ways. Or you may prefer independent work because you find other voices distracting and learn better by delving into your own thought process.

Early in your college career, you should try to understand your own learning preferences and tendencies because then you can better determine which academic situations will allow you to thrive and which may be more challenging. You can use various rubrics to help you better understand yourself. The two that we will examine in this chapter are VARK and the Myers-Briggs Type Indicator. By understanding your learning preferences, you can determine what you can do to help yourself excel during your college years.

What Is VARK?

VARK stands for Visual, Aural, Read/Write, and Kinesthetic. The VARK questionnaire helps people understand their learning preferences based on these four sensory modalities. Specifically, it sheds light on how people prefer to digest information and communicate their learning. Some students highly prefer just one of the four sensory modalities, but other students are multimodal—that is, they prefer two or more sensory modalities. For example, a student might have a strong preference for both the Visual modality and the Aural modality.

VARK is described in more detail later in this chapter, but before you can understand your learning profile, you need to determine your VARK preferences. Take the test online at www.vark-learn.com/english/page .asp?p=questionnaire.

Understanding VARK

Once you have taken the VARK test, you receive a score that tabulates how many questions you answered that correspond to each sensory modality. For example, your score might look like this:

Visual: 4

Aural: 3

Read/Write: 8

Kinesthetic: 1

In this case, Read/Write is your preferred learning preference, given the number of questions you answered that tie to the Read/Write modality. If, however, your scorecard indicates two modalities with similar scores (for example, Visual: 6; Aural: 7; Read/Write: 2; Kinesthetic: 1), you are multimodal and prefer two sensory modalities almost equally. Let's define each modality so that you can understand how to use your VARK score in the classroom and while studying.

Visual (V). The Visual modality is a preference for visual representations, including images such as charts, graphs, diagrams, photographs, maps, symbols such as arrows and circles, and other visual illustrations that show patterns or shapes. Those with a visual preference are not necessarily drawn to words that are written on a board with just a shape around them. Instead, they prefer symbols used to *connect* the words in some meaningful way.

Aural (A). The Aural modality focuses on listening, or what can be heard or spoken. Those with an aural preference find it easier to digest and understand information by listening. They learn well through lectures, speaking out loud, group and class discussions, and Web conferences. Visual representations or written materials are not as helpful. Students with this preference often talk to themselves while studying, speaking information in their own words for easier learning.

Some of your college courses may not fit your learning style; when this happens, try to be flexible. Think creatively about how you can incorporate your learning style in a way that is appropriate and helpful, possibly by engaging with the material in a meaningful way after class.

Read/Write (R). The Read/Write modality is all about words. People with this preference learn better through the written word—whether it's the act of writing or the act of reading. Not surprisingly, instructors and students often prefer this type of learning, given how much emphasis the academic world places on the written word.

Kinesthetic (K). The Kinesthetic modality is a preference for hands-on, real-world learning with a physical component, such as personal experiences, vivid examples, or simulated or real practice. Kinesthetic learners want to *do* something to learn a concept, such as an experiment, or prefer to see a live demonstration in order to experience the learning in a concrete way. Students with a kinesthetic preference learn better when they engage one or more of their senses.

I Know My VARK Score: Now What?

Once you receive your VARK score and understand which sensory modalities you prefer, you need to learn how to put your preferences to work for you in college. When choosing classes and instructors, for example, you may perform better when the style of teaching and assignments are more in line with your learning preference. However, you can't pick only classes that match your learning style, so you need to learn how to adapt. And to help you improve your test and quiz scores, you can find strategies for studying that can be tailored to your learning preferences.

Choose classes that align with your preferences. In college, you can't pick every course you take, but you can choose many of your classes, even within college requirements. When picking classes, be sure to consider your VARK learning preference. If a class fits your learning style, you will stay more engaged and will learn better. For example, if you are an auditory learner, try to choose discussion-based courses; the audible back-and-forth of class conversation will aid your learning. If you are a kinesthetic learner, you might do particularly well in courses that provide opportunities for hands-on work, such as science classes with labs.

QUICK TIP

Match Teaching and Learning Styles
While assessing which class to choose, determine whether an instructor's teaching style fits your VARK learning preference. For example, if you have a visual preference, try to find an instructor who relies heavily on visual representations to relay information during lectures. If you have a reading/writing preference, look for an instructor who gives mostly reading- and writing-based assignments. Students who have taken the class or your advisor can often provide a useful perspective on the instructor's teaching methods and assignments.

Learn to adapt. You will have to take a number of college courses that don't align with your learning style, so it's important to find ways to adapt. One good strategy is to take class notes in a way that draws on your preferences. For example, if you have a visual preference, use visual representations in your notes; if you are an auditory learner, read your notes out loud after class. When you are learning course material, try to make use of your VARK preference. For example, if you are a kinesthetic learner, try to engage several of your five senses in the material by developing your own experiment or personalizing the material. If you have a reading/writing preference, look for additional readings on the course's subject matter.

Use preference-specific study techniques. Studying in college is complicated because there are so many ways to study and so many different types of classes to study for. To increase your understanding of material and to improve your test scores, determine what study techniques might complement your VARK preferences.

Here are examples for each VARK sensory modality:

- **Visual.** While studying, have a pen and paper handy to draw visual representations of the information you're learning. Find ways to represent the information with symbols and diagrams. Even while reading, draw symbols in the text so that you can turn the reading into your own visual masterpiece.

- **Aural.** As you study material, talk out loud, either to yourself or with others. The more you hear or speak the information, the more likely you are to retain it. When you speak the information, make the material your own by using your own words or phrasing. You might want to form study groups in which group members quiz each other on material verbally or through conversations. To make the most of your aural preference, record lectures and then play them back while you are studying.

- **Read/Write.** Write down meaningful words as you study. Take many notes in your own words while you are studying lectures and readings. Similarly, while doing your readings, write notes in the margins that highlight important points. Marginal notes will help you think about the material and will provide a word guide to refer to later on when studying the reading for a test.

- **Kinesthetic.** Figure out ways to learn in a more hands-on fashion. For example, to deepen your understanding, think of real-world examples that tie directly to the information you are studying. Meet with an instructor to help you personalize the material. Find ways to engage several of your senses in the material, such as doing an experiment yourself.

✓ CHECKLIST FOR HOW TO USE YOUR LEARNING STYLE TO YOUR BENEFIT

- ☐ Try to find classes that fit your learning preferences.
- ☐ Take notes in ways that draw on your learning style.
- ☐ Use study techniques that complement your learning preferences.
- ☐ When classes don't fit your learning preferences, find ways of incorporating your learning style into assignments or study techniques.

What If I Am Multimodal?

If you prefer two or more of the VARK sensory modalities, you might have an easier time finding classes and instructors that fit your preferences. And you can engage

Visual Walkthrough

Use Your VARK Learning Preference during Study Sessions

While studying for tests, draw on your VARK learning preferences to increase your understanding and retention of material. To better retain the information in this reading, follow the suggestions for your particular learning style.

process for food, clothing, building materials, and many other purposes. Most likely, these first Americans wandered into the Western Hemisphere more or less accidentally, hungry and in pursuit of their prey.

African and Asian Origins

Human beings lived elsewhere in the world for hundreds of thousands of years before they reached the Western Hemisphere. They lacked a way to travel to the Western Hemisphere because millions of years before humans existed anywhere on the globe, North and South America became detached from the gigantic common landmass scientists now call Pangaea. About 240 million years ago, powerful forces deep within the earth fractured Pangaea and slowly pushed continents apart to approximately their present positions (Map 1.1). This process of continental drift encircled the land of the Western Hemisphere with large oceans that isolated it from the other continents long before early human beings (*Homo erectus*) first appeared in Africa about two million years ago. (Hereafter in this chapter, the abbreviation *BP* — archaeologists' notation for "years before the present" — is used to indicate dates earlier than two thousand years ago. Dates more recent than two thousand years ago are indicated with the common and familiar notation *AD* — for example, AD 1492.)

More than 1.5 million years after *Homo erectus* appeared, or about 400,000 BP, modern humans (*Homo sapiens*) evolved in Africa. All human beings throughout

MAP 1.1
Continental Drift
Massive geological forces separated North and South America from other continents eons before human beings evolved in Africa 1.5 million years ago.

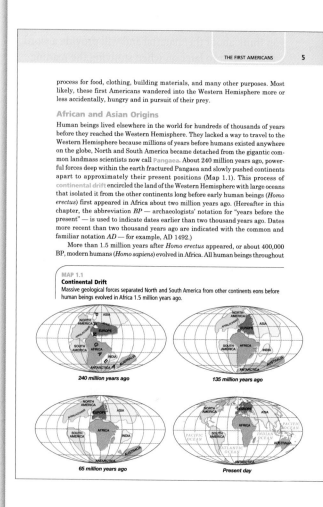

240 million years ago

135 million years ago

65 million years ago

Present day

- **Visual learners.** Draw a timeline re-creating important information in the maps, and include relevant details from the text.

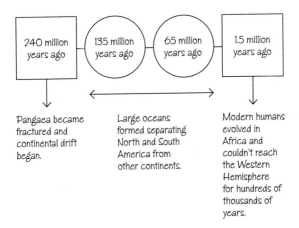

| 240 million years ago | 135 million years ago | 65 million years ago | 1.5 million years ago |

Pangaea became fractured and continental drift began.

Large oceans formed separating North and South America from other continents.

Modern humans evolved in Africa and couldn't reach the Western Hemisphere for hundreds of thousands of years.

- **Aural learners.** Read the important details of the text out loud, discuss the material with an instructor during office hours, and ask study group members to quiz you on the material.

- **Read/Write learners.** Write your understanding of the material in your own words:

  "Modern humans evolved 1.5 million years ago in Africa, and because continents drifted apart long before humans existed (continental drift began 240 million years ago), humans didn't set foot anywhere in the Western Hemisphere for hundreds of thousands of years. Humans didn't have a way to travel across the vast oceans that separated North and South America from the rest of the continents (these oceans formed over the course of millions of years—between 65 and 135 million years ago)."

- **Kinesthetic learners.** To engage several senses, ask an instructor for a movie that illustrates the concepts detailed in the reading. Or demonstrate the continental drift shown in Map 1.1 in a concrete way: create different continents out of clay, and move them at million-year intervals in a pan of water, representing the oceans separating North and South America from the other continents.

in class and study for tests using techniques that incorporate all of your favored modalities. You might try a few different ways of taking notes in class and find that one works better for you. Or certain note-taking strategies might work better depending on the type of class you're taking. Similarly, while studying, you might learn more effectively if you use specific styles of studying that are tailored to different types of classes.

Whatever the case, understanding your VARK preferences can help you succeed in college: either you can tailor your class choices and study techniques in order to target these preferences, or you can find ways to adapt to classes that don't speak to your preferences.

CASE STUDY

Audrey explains how her learning preferences affect her college experience.

I learn most effectively and have the most rewarding experiences in classes that fit my learning style in one way or another. I prefer an intimate classroom setting where I can actively interact with the instructor and other students, via discussions, team collaboration, and group projects, instead of sitting through a long lecture in which information has to be absorbed passively without an active exchange of ideas. But I've gotten a lot out of lectures by taking notes in a more visual way that keeps my brain more engaged and improves my understanding of the material.

For subjects that require lectures and presentations without much chance for interaction, I find myself the most engaged by visuals. And for those classes that don't fit my learning style, being able to apply class materials to a subject of personal interest helps a lot.

Even though these learning styles often don't apply to every course because of the nature of the subject, I have learned that seeking out classes that fit at least one of my learning styles makes the learning experience all the more pleasant and often influences my performance in a positive way.

QUESTIONS FOR REFLECTION: Are you taking classes that don't fit your learning style? If so, how are you performing in these classes? Can you think of ways to draw on your learning preferences to improve your performance?

What Is Myers-Briggs?

The Myers-Briggs Type Indicator (MBTI) is another instrument that can help you understand your learning preferences. The MBTI identifies the different aspects of your personality that define who you are and how you interact with others. Knowing your MBTI personality type can clarify the ways in which you prefer to learn and can help you make informed choices in college that can lead to improved academic performance.

Similar to the VARK questionnaire, the MBTI test reveals your personal preferences based on your responses to a series of questions. There are no right or wrong answers—you are merely indicating your personal preferences. The MBTI has four scales, each of which has two classifications:

1. Extraversion (E) or Introversion (I)
2. Sensing (S) or Intuition (N)
3. Thinking (T) or Feeling (F)
4. Judging (J) or Perceiving (P)

The MBTI test results will indicate that you have a moderate or strong preference for one of the two classifications within each scale. Sixteen different combinations or personality types are possible:

ISTJ	ISTP	ESTP	ESTJ
ISFJ	ISFP	ESFP	ESFJ
INFJ	INFP	ENFP	ENFJ
INTJ	INTP	ENTP	ENTJ

For example, you might have a personality type that tends toward Extraversion, Sensing, Thinking, and Judging (ESTJ). The MBTI test will indicate where you rank in each classification. You might have a very strong tendency toward Extraversion and demonstrate little tendency toward Introversion. But you might fall somewhere in the middle on the Thinking/Feeling scale, with Thinking tendencies just slightly outweighing Feeling tendencies.

Taking the MBTI test is the best way to determine your personality type, but you can get a general sense of your MBTI personality type by reading the brief descriptions of each classification in the next section. Professionals must be certified to administer, score, and interpret the MBTI test properly, and several Web sites provide this service, usually for a fee. Some colleges offer opportunities to take the MBTI test, often through the Career Services Office (or equivalent office).

QUICK TIP

Take the MBTI

If your college does not offer the MBTI test, go to the Myers & Briggs Foundation Web site (www.myersbriggs .org/my-mbti-personality-type/take-the-mbti-instrument /index.asp) to find other ways to access the test.

Personality Type Can Influence College Choices

Once you understand the definition of each Myers-Briggs classification, you can determine how to use this information to assist your learning throughout college. Knowing your Myers-Briggs preferences can help you make informed decisions about classes and study strategies.

Extraversion versus Introversion.   This scale indicates how people prefer to interact with the outside world. Extraverts gain energy not only from being around people but also from being actively engaged with them. At the other end of the spectrum, Introversion is a tendency to look inward. Introverts gain energy from thinking about ideas inside their head and value and seek time alone.

- **Extraverts** enjoy classes that allow for active class participation and group discussions because they are comfortable speaking in groups and are stimulated in these situations. They prefer instructors who facilitate lively and active discussions and debates. In addition, they seek opportunities to work on group projects because their learning is enhanced in the presence of others. Extraverts might want to form study groups so that they can study in an interactive rather than a passive setting.

- **Introverts** tend to be drawn to classes that allow for deep introspection and individual work. They prefer instructors who lecture without too much class discussion; opportunities to speak one-on-one with instructors; and assignments that focus on individual thought rather than group collaboration. Given their tendency to get lost in their thoughts, introverts tend to study in ways that allow them to process information without interruption from others.

Sensing versus Intuition.   Sensing types and intuitive types differ greatly in how they interpret, digest, and analyze information. Those with a Sensing preference are detail-oriented pragmatists who use the five senses and focus on physical reality and facts, things that are real, and things that can be seen, heard, and felt. Those with a preference for Intuition, by contrast, look beyond physical reality to the meaning that can be interpreted. They believe that "gut feelings" and "intuition" matter more than what can be gathered from the five senses.

- **Sensing** types are often interested in courses that are fact-based and have practical applications, such as science, math, and economics. They prefer learning opportunities and assignments that draw on all five senses, such as experiments, labs, and experiential learning. They benefit from study techniques that involve processing information through multiple senses, such as redoing hands-on experiments or forming study groups that engage the senses of hearing and seeing.

- **Intuitive** types are drawn to classes that offer open-ended discussions and to assignments that allow them to unravel the meaning behind concepts and ideas. They like to focus on big-picture topics. While studying, they enjoy finding ways to personalize the material by bringing in personal reactions and experiences.

Thinking versus Feeling.   These two classifications differ in the way decisions are made and what factors are important in making decisions. Thinking types analyze the pros and cons of a situation and try to weigh both sides fairly, without letting emotion get in the way. Thinkers value logic and rational analysis of facts. Feeling types, however, tend to make decisions with their heart, rather than with their head. They try to understand how their decisions will affect other people because they want to do what's best for those involved.

- **Thinking** types prefer classes that require analytical skills. Thinkers want to apply general principles and rules whenever possible. They seek out instructors who value and reward this type of thinking and who give assignments that ask students to look at both sides of an issue using logic, rather than emotion. They learn best when they can test their understanding by applying rules or logic to novel problems and situations, rather than merely memorizing.

- **Feeling** types often excel in classes that provide opportunities to understand and think about how people are affected by situations and events. They particularly enjoy subjects such as psychology, sociology, and history. Feelers like to make judgments with their hearts, so they are drawn to instructors who value analysis that brings in personal emotions and reactions. When trying to understand and remember important concepts, they do best if they can think of examples that involve people in a meaningful way.

Judging versus Perceiving. This scale indicates how people prefer to structure their life. Judging does not refer to being judgmental. Rather, those with a Judging tendency, according to the MBTI definition, have a preference for making decisions. Judging types find comfort when things are settled, in order, and planned rather than left uncertain. By contrast, perceiving types like to stay flexible and spontaneous, taking in information readily and easily. They want to be more open to what might or might not happen.

- **Judging** types prefer well-organized classes with clear guidelines and predictable deadlines. They appreciate instructors who present information in a clear and concise way and who stick to an outline. Judging types prefer very detailed syllabi and clearly defined, unambiguous assignments. When they study, judging types usually begin with a clearly laid-out to-do list.

- **Perceiving** types are usually drawn to classes that allow for a certain amount of freedom and creativity. They seek out instructors who are flexible and who don't mind deviating from the syllabus. Perceiving types prefer classes without clear right or wrong answers so that they can explore all angles of a problem without boundaries. They enjoy studying in an environment that is constantly changing (such as a student center) and that allows creativity to flow.

---

⑤ WAYS TO MAKE THE MOST OF CLASSES THAT DON'T FIT YOUR MBTI TYPE

1. Study in ways that fit your learning preferences.

    Finding opportunities to use your learning preferences to your advantage will likely increase your understanding of material and your performance in the class.

2. Talk to your instructor about how you can draw on aspects of your MBTI type in and outside of class.

    Let your instructor know that you want to do all you can to succeed. Your instructor may have suggestions for how you can draw on your learning style in meaningful ways.

3. Find ways to approach assignments that draw on your learning style.

    Consider whether your learning style might help you approach assignments more creatively and in ways that can improve your performance.

4. Talk with students who have taken the class to find out what aided and impeded their class performance.

    Don't underestimate the power of learning from your peers. Their insight can be invaluable, since they usually are honest and forthright about their experiences.

5. Consult with the Academic Advising Office or work with a tutor to develop strategies that can help you succeed.

    You may struggle in a class that doesn't draw on your strengths, so don't hesitate to get help from experts in the field or from campus supports.

Self-Knowledge Is Power

The VARK and Myers-Briggs tests can help you understand your personal tendencies. They are powerful tools, especially if this self-knowledge allows you to make better academic choices and to develop study techniques that are suited to your preferences. When you consider your preferences, however, remember that they are not set in stone and that none are "good" or "bad." No judgment is attached to any VARK preference or Myers-Briggs personality type.

These preferences are on a continuum and can be influenced by situations and circumstances. So, while you might be strong on Extraversion, you might also crave time alone to think, just like those with a tendency for Introversion.

Think of rubrics like VARK and Myers-Briggs as a starting point. Although they give you a good sense of who you are, don't let them define you. Be thoughtful about when your preferences and personality type matter the most, because you won't always have the chance to make choices that are in line with these tendencies.

QUICK TIP

Expand Your Horizons

College is a time to expand your horizons, so don't be afraid to take classes that don't fit your learning preferences, especially if you are interested in the subject matter. Stepping out of your comfort zone allows for growth and will help you develop skills and strategies to succeed in situations that might be uncomfortable. You will experience many uncomfortable situations in college and after college, so being willing to take a risk and learning how to adapt is an important life skill.

In college, you'll have to take classes that don't fit your learning style, and you'll have to work with instructors whose personality type doesn't match your own. Now, however, you have tools to better understand different ways of being in and interacting with the world. This understanding can help you see multiple perspectives so that you can adapt to uncomfortable situations. And you might even find that you need to develop behavior patterns that don't come naturally, good practice for life after college when you'll face similar challenges.

Critical Thinking
in College

It's likely that at some point in your life a teacher has asked you to "think critically" or to use "critical thinking skills." But what does the term *critical thinking* really mean? According to Dictionary.com, *critical thinking* is defined as "the mental process of actively and skillfully conceptualizing, applying, analyzing, synthesizing, and evaluating information to reach an answer or conclusion." This is a thorough definition, but it might sound a bit overwhelming. Don't worry, however. Critical thinking can come naturally if you practice *how* to be a critical thinker.

Critical Thinking in College

All aspects of college academic life—attending lectures, visiting instructors during office hours, completing assignments, working in study groups—require that you use critical thinking skills. College instructors expect that you will think more critically and carefully than you ever have before. Simply regurgitating what you read in textbooks or what you hear during lectures is not enough. Instructors want students to think freely and analytically, to ask questions and offer a fresh perspective, and to be willing to think outside the box. What instructors want is critical thinking.

In fact, critical thinking is at the core of a college education. Colleges are in the business of educating for many reasons. One important reason is to help students become active and engaged citizens of our society. To be truly active and engaged in a job, within a local or global community, in a school system, in politics, or in any other arena, people must think deeply about whatever information and experiences they encounter. Colleges want students to develop critical thinking skills so that they can evaluate information and their experiences by exercising careful judgment, offering novel insights and ideas, challenging the status quo, and asking insightful questions—essential life skills.

Five Steps for Critical Thinking

To become a critical thinker in college, you need to develop certain traits that characterize this type of deep thinking. The following five steps will help you make critical thinking a natural reflex. You might want to refer back to this list periodically, whenever you encounter a new academic situation.

Step 1: Ask a lot of questions (and answer them!).
Asking questions is a key aspect of critical thinking. Asking and answering questions will help you clarify details, clear up confusion, and push for a deeper understanding of the material. When you ask questions, the material will become more meaningful because the questions you ask will matter to you. Asking questions will also help you remember the information. Why? Asking thoughtful questions means that you're a thinking and engaged participant rather than a passive observer.

For example, as you're reading material or listening to a lecture, continually ask if you understand what is being argued or presented. If not, ask yourself what is causing your confusion, and get answers. In a class debate, ask your classmates what evidence they have for the arguments they're making. During an instructor's office hours, explain why you think the assigned readings complement or contradict one another; then ask whether your instructor agrees or disagrees with your assessment.

Step 2: Evaluate your own reactions.   Do you agree or disagree with the information being presented? Why? This type of evaluation pushes your thinking to a deep and personal level. By critically evaluating your reaction to the material, you're asking yourself not only whether an argument makes sense but also whether you believe it. Whether you agree or disagree, it's important to ask yourself why.

For example, do you think your instructor's lecture was compelling? If you agree with the instructor's arguments, ask yourself what evidence convinced you and why. If you disagree, ask yourself what evidence was suspect and why. If you don't fully understand or agree with your instructor's arguments, what additional

"You're the best teacher I've ever had. You opened my eyes to the world and showed me how to think critically... I was *happy* until I met *you*."

▲

Remember to stay in tune with your instructor's expectations as you engage in critical thinking. Be a critical thinker who offers a novel perspective, constantly analyzes material, and asks insightful questions, but also understand what you need to do to succeed in the class. If you need some help with critical thinking, talk to your instructor.

questions should you ask? What do you need to do to dig deeper into the topic and come to a conclusion? Meeting with your instructor during office hours is a great opportunity to exercise your critical thinking.

Step 3: Analyze the information with a "critical" lens.
During lectures or when you read, try to poke holes in the argument and ask whether anything is missing. Has any evidence or information been forgotten, covered up, or ignored? College is your chance to be thoughtfully skeptical about what you're hearing and reading. Obviously, you won't be able to poke holes in a number of things—laws of physics, mathematical theorems,

well-proven theories. However, no academic discipline is a perfect science. College is the time to push back and be thoughtful about the information you encounter.

For example, after you analyze aspects of the information presented during a lecture, do you think important material was left out, oversimplified, or minimized? Would different examples or evidence have altered your understanding of the instructor's argument or perspective? If you're skeptical of aspects of a lecture, why do you think that's the case? Do readings offer a diverse or complementary perspective that clarifies your thinking?

Step 4: Make connections and keep the big picture in mind. You're bombarded with a lot of information in college. To be an effective critical thinker, take the time to step back periodically and synthesize what you're learning in order to see the big picture. Synthesizing— or combining different aspects of the information in a coherent and meaningful way—while also making connections between different types of material can clarify what is most important.

For example, connect your instructor's lectures with what you're reading in the class. Instructors assign readings for a reason. By thinking critically about why the readings are important and how they relate to the instructor's lectures, you're expanding your understanding of the material in important ways. You might realize that a reading's argument differs from the instructor's position on the subject. Which side makes more sense to you and why? The key is to apply what you're learning in the class's various components—lectures, readings, and assignments—to the bigger picture of the course as a whole.

Step 5: Apply your learning to your own life experiences. All of us are shaped by our past learning and experiences. The more you can bring your past experiences into the college learning process, the more powerful your critical thinking skills will be. If you personalize material and make it matter to you, you're more likely to think deeply.

For example, consider how your past shapes the way you look at information, the reasons you agree with certain aspects of an argument, or why you have specific types of questions. Did a past class significantly influence your thinking on the topic? If so, why? Have you had any experiences—travel, activities, internships, jobs—that have shaped your perspectives? Asking *why* the material is important to you is an interesting question to answer.

QUICK TIP

Bring "You" into the Equation

If you're taking a required class that you didn't choose, try to figure out how the material is relevant to your life. By bringing "you" into the equation, you will care more, think more deeply, and perform more successfully.

The five steps in this process are in no particular order. You may (and should) ask questions while you think critically about information. Or you may simultaneously evaluate your reaction to material and consider how the past informs your thinking. You don't have to do the steps in any strict sequence; rather, this five-step process is intended as a guide you can use to further develop your skills as a critical thinker.

✓ CRITICAL THINKING CHECKLIST

- ☐ **Conceptualize** material fully by asking questions frequently and finding answers.
- ☐ **Evaluate** your reaction to material by asking whether you agree or disagree with it and why.
- ☐ **Analyze** material by being critical of all perspectives and by asking what is missing.
- ☐ **Synthesize** material to make connections and examine the big picture.
- ☐ **Apply** what you're learning to past experiences in order to better understand your reactions to material.

Q CASE STUDY

Maryann shares her perspective on developing critical thinking skills in college.

Once I arrived at college, I realized that my courses required more in-depth analysis and interpretations than I was used to and that I had to adjust my critical thinking skills. I discovered that the ways I used to read and write were going to have to change drastically. As an avid reader and highlighter fanatic, I quickly realized writing my "philosophical" college essays required more than just taking extensive marginal notes. I had to really think, immerse myself in the material, and redraft my conclusions as my analysis of the evidence changed.

My critical thinking skills continue to develop each day, adjusting to different aspects of my social and academic life. And I've realized that critical thinkers are in search of "a truth," while also understanding that there are many ways in which to interpret things. Also, when you are using critical thinking skills, whether you're writing an essay or participating in discussions in class, there is no specific road map to follow because everyone comes at the material from different perspectives. And it does help to become passionate about something because the way in which you use your thinking skills will be grounded in your personal beliefs, making the material matter more.

QUESTIONS FOR REFLECTION: Is the level of critical thinking required in your college courses different from what was expected of you in high school? Do you understand how to be more critical in your thinking? If you're not sure, talk with your advisor, your instructors, or the Academic Advising Office to get help.

Try Not to Inhibit Critical Thinking

Engaging in critical thinking isn't easy. Students sometimes hold beliefs that inhibit or limit their critical thinking. For example, it's natural to assume that your instructor or a textbook author knows everything and that you don't know anything. As a result, you might tend to be a passive observer during lectures and while you read, taking everything as fact. But agreeing with everything prevents you from thinking critically about the information presented. It's fine to agree, but ask yourself *why* you agree and whether you have found enough evidence to support your decision to agree.

Another common pitfall is ignoring your reaction to the material presented because you assume that it doesn't matter if you agree or not. However, not only is your perspective valuable, but it is also a new one. Sharing and understanding your reactions to material will enhance your thinking and might even influence other students, creating a more meaningful learning experience.

Moreover, try to ask any questions you have, even if you're afraid of looking foolish. It's easy to feel intimidated in college, especially as a first-year student, but if you're not asking questions, you're not engaging in critical thinking. At the very least, ask questions one-on-one during your instructor's office hours or with peers you trust.

QUICK TIP

Think For Yourself

When you work with a study group, be sure to think as an individual. It's easy to assume that the groupthink that arises out of your study group discussion is the only way to think about an issue. However, don't let the group limit your own critical thinking, especially if you feel unsettled by conclusions that the study group makes.

Where to Use Your Critical Thinking Skills

The five steps for critical thinking, although general, can be applied to all of your academic experiences in college. Try using the five steps, in any order, while reading class assignments, completing problem sets, researching and writing papers, participating in group projects, and listening to lectures. Instructors will expect you to think critically in each of these academic endeavors, so take note of the specific ways critical thinking can be applied to reading, writing, informational literacy, and note-taking in the chapters that follow.

In addition to academics, you can apply your critical thinking skills to everyday college life—when you are solving problems or making decisions and throughout any creative process.

Critical Thinking While Problem Solving

Good problem solving depends on critical thinking, so keep in mind a few rules of thumb when you're trying to solve a problem. First, understand the root of the problem; next, gather and analyze any information to help you solve the problem; and finally, brainstorm all possible solutions to the problem before determining which solutions are best.

Understand the root of the problem. Take the time to determine where the problem is coming from. What exactly are you trying to solve? For example, if you're having an academic problem in a class and want to figure out what to do, consider all the possible roots of the problem. Are you struggling to understand the professor's lectures, get through all the assigned readings, or finish timed tests? By uncovering the roots of the problem, you'll be more likely to find the right solution.

Gather and analyze information. Determine what would assist you when solving the problem. Let's say the root of your academic problem is difficulty completing

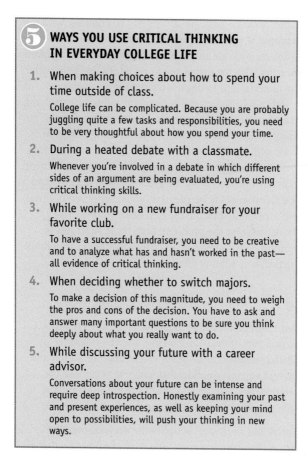

⑤ WAYS YOU USE CRITICAL THINKING IN EVERYDAY COLLEGE LIFE

1. **When making choices about how to spend your time outside of class.**

   College life can be complicated. Because you are probably juggling quite a few tasks and responsibilities, you need to be very thoughtful about how you spend your time.

2. **During a heated debate with a classmate.**

   Whenever you're involved in a debate in which different sides of an argument are being evaluated, you're using critical thinking skills.

3. **While working on a new fundraiser for your favorite club.**

   To have a successful fundraiser, you need to be creative and to analyze what has and hasn't worked in the past—all evidence of critical thinking.

4. **When deciding whether to switch majors.**

   To make a decision of this magnitude, you need to weigh the pros and cons of the decision. You have to ask and answer many important questions to be sure you think deeply about what you really want to do.

5. **While discussing your future with a career advisor.**

   Conversations about your future can be intense and require deep introspection. Honestly examining your past and present experiences, as well as keeping your mind open to possibilities, will push your thinking in new ways.

tests in the time allotted. During your information gathering, you find that most other students are not struggling to finish tests. And you recognize that in the past you have had trouble with timed tests, particularly in the same subject. You also often get stuck on a few problems and then go blank, making it difficult to complete the remainder of the test. Analyzing this information helps you recognize that the tests aren't unusually long because others are completing them in time; rather, you realize that you're struggling to understand aspects of the material and are experiencing test anxiety.

Brainstorm all possible solutions. To continue with our example, if you think carefully about your analysis of the problem, you can find many possible solutions, including meeting with the instructor to get additional help with the material and to discuss test-taking strategies. Another solution might be to spend more time studying. Maybe you decide it would be worthwhile to form a study group, visit your Academic Advising Office, or work with a tutor.

With possible solutions in mind, use your judgment to determine which one would work best. If more than one solution could be effective, you might even use trial and error to determine the best one. However you choose to solve the problem, keep these strategies in mind to help you engage in critical thinking throughout the problem-solving process.

Critical Thinking When Making Decisions

Similar to problem solving, critical thinking is a fundamental part of decision making, and the rules are similar—clarify the decision you're making; gather and analyze any information that will help you make the decision; brainstorm and weigh the pros and cons of each possible alternative before deciding what to do.

Clarify the decision. Simplify the decision-making process by stripping away aspects of the decision that are irrelevant. For example, if you're trying to pick a major, think about the fields you are *not* interested in. Then you'll be left with the majors that are relevant—making your decision easier and clearer.

Gather and analyze information. Let's say you conclude that you're most interested in majoring in psychology, sociology, or English. Then, determine what information will help you differentiate among these three majors. For example, how many classes in each major sound particularly interesting? What makes the classes interesting? If class size matters to you, check how many students will be taking the various classes, because some majors tend to have larger classes than others. Talk to fellow students majoring in each field, as well as instructors, to get a better feel for the majors. And consider how your own career aspirations might influence your decision.

Weigh the pros and cons. Keeping in mind the information you have gathered, list and then weigh the pros and cons of each possible option. To continue with our example, if you conclude that the average class size in the Psychology Department is larger than you prefer but that you're more interested in the psychology classes and have learned about exciting research opportunities you'd like to pursue, majoring in psychology might be the right decision. If you also realize that you are nearly as interested in English as in psychology, you might decide to pursue English as a minor.

Whatever the case, remember to engage your critical thinking skills throughout the decision-making process. When you engage in this type of thorough thinking, you'll be more satisfied with your decision.

QUICK TIP

Take Time to Reflect
Take time to reflect after you've chosen a solution to your problem or made a decision. Continue to be a critical thinker by evaluating how things are going. Is your solution working? If so, why is it working? If not, should you consider other solutions to the problem? After making a decision, are you happy with it? If not, can you change your decision to make things better?

Critical Thinking and Creativity

You might wonder why the concept of creativity is relevant in a chapter about critical thinking. In fact, creativity and critical thinking are intricately linked. You need to be creative when engaging in aspects of critical thinking such as coming up with examples that clarify an idea, trying to poke holes in a well-supported argument, or developing new or alternative explanations. And critical thinking is essential when you are being creative because as you come up with novel ideas or explanations during the creative process, you need to analyze whether the ideas and explanations make sense, can be well supported, and are relevant.

In college, you can be creative in many ways—while writing a paper, working on a group project, organizing a club event, engaging in research, debating a topic, or discussing a lecture with an instructor. Think critically throughout any creative process by taking the time to question, analyze, and evaluate what you are creating. And when you engage in critical thinking, don't lose sight of the power of creativity in improving and expanding your thought process.

Chapter 5
Note-Taking

It's the second week of class, and you're sitting in Economics 101 with laptop in hand for extensive note-taking. The instructor begins to lecture, and you start taking notes. But how do you listen and take notes at the same time? Is it better to write down everything word-for-word and then later figure out what the instructor said? What if you can't get everything down? Are notes all that useful anyway?

Even though note-taking isn't easy, it is important. Notes help you make sense of what you're learning by pulling together concepts and revealing your instructor's perspective on the subject. Notes are an invaluable study tool, and you can constantly refer back to them. Moreover, you'll need notes to study from and often to complete assignments. In college, you'll need to develop the skill of taking *useful* notes, which involves a great deal of critical thinking.

Take Thoughtful Notes

Many students assume that critical thinking is relevant to readings and assignments, but not to other academic situations. For example, you might view lectures as a time to sit back and just listen, taking notes on whatever the instructor says but not thinking critically about the lecture. When you sit passively, though, it's easy to lose focus, making it difficult to recognize whether you truly understand what's being said. Once the class is over, you move on to your next activity and don't give a second thought to the material presented in the lecture.

In college, the information presented during class is integral to your learning and to your academic success, so it's important to be thoughtfully engaged during class. College instructors expect that students will think carefully and deeply about the material and perspectives that are presented and about any noteworthy research. Note-taking is a way to stay actively engaged, but taking thoughtful notes is possible only if you can fully concentrate throughout class.

Set the Scene

To help yourself concentrate and stay engaged, try to set
yourself up for success. Be sure to complete assigned
readings before each lecture so that you are familiar with
what will be discussed. Being prepared will help you stay
more focused because you have already mulled over
topics and issues that might be discussed during class.

Another way to prepare for a lecture is to ask
yourself big-picture questions: Where does today's topic
fit into the wider themes of the class? Is this lecture a
continuation of something that was discussed previously,
or will the information be new? Do I already know
something about the material being presented?

---

5 WAYS SMART STUDENTS STAY ALERT DURING CLASS

1. **Bring snacks to eat, especially during three-hour marathon classes.**

   It's difficult to fall asleep with food in your mouth.

2. **Turn off phone alerts, close e-mail, and hide Facebook.**

   Distractions that are this tempting can rapidly diminish your concentration. To keep your brain focused, turn off any devices that might sidetrack you during class.

3. **Sit closer to the instructor and away from classmates who might distract you.**

   The closer you are to the instructor, the more likely you are to listen carefully and concentrate on the lecture, making it more difficult to get drawn into any classmate drama.

4. **Reenergize your body whenever possible— breathe deeply, move your shoulders, unobtrusively move your legs up and down.**

   Keeping your blood flowing will help your brain stay more alert. And when your body is moving, it's almost impossible to fall asleep!

5. **Take notes in your own words using one of the note-taking formats described in this chapter.**

   Taking notes forces you to listen, think, and write—tasks that will increase your focus and understanding.

Determine what distractions hinder your learning in class so that you can eliminate them. If you tend to fall asleep in class, figure out what will help you stay awake. Or maybe you get restless in class and sometimes feel as though you want to get up and walk around. If so, think of ways you can subtly release your energy without distracting other students.

It's not always possible to stay focused when you need to. Maybe you're dealing with a family problem, or you heard some exciting news and can't wait to celebrate. If something distracting causes you to lose your focus in class, be proactive: ask a classmate if you can borrow his or her class notes, or visit your instructor during office hours. If you find that being distracted is a chronic problem, something more serious might be going on. Don't hesitate to get help from your advisor or someone in the Academic Advising Office.

QUICK TIP

Clear Your Head

Unexpectedly, you can be confronted with difficult life situations, making it tough to concentrate on anything. When this happens, take a few minutes before class to write down what's on your mind and what actions you might take to deal with the issue. This technique allows you to express your emotions, while freeing your brain to focus on what's going on in class.

View Lectures as Conversations

A useful technique for taking thoughtful notes in class is to pretend that each lecture is a conversation between you and the instructor. If you view the lecture as an exchange of ideas and thoughts, you become an *active* and *important* participant, rather than a passive observer. Your notes, then, are a place to write down your "lecture conversation." But what exactly should you write down?

Capture the main ideas. Write down the main ideas and important takeaways that are presented in class, including any opinions, perspectives, or research the instructor discusses.

Write down examples, evidence, and anecdotes.
These details will shed more light on the material being discussed and will help you better understand it.

Highlight anything the instructor repeats. Whenever your instructor emphasizes certain points by repeating or summarizing them, be sure to write them down in your notes—this is information your instructor wants you to remember.

React to the information. Do you agree or disagree with what the instructor is saying? Why? What is your opinion on the material? Does the information presented make sense to you? Is anything missing? Throughout the lecture, write down your analysis or evaluation of the material your instructor is presenting.

Determine what questions you have. In your notes, write down any questions you have about the material presented in the lecture. After class, get answers to these questions from your instructor, or discuss the questions with your study group.

QUICK TIP

Use Your Own Words
You don't need to write down every word the instructor utters. In fact, if you merely transcribe a lecture, you are only passively engaging in the class. You're so busy writing down every word that you're not thinking critically about what's being said. Instead, try to take notes using your own words.

Writing down your personal reactions, analysis, and questions in your notes will keep you more engaged because you are responding to the lecture conversation that is unfolding throughout the class. To make any conversation meaningful, you need to listen actively and then ponder, react, and ask questions along the way. Unlike a conversation you might have with a friend, though, this exchange of ideas and questions happens in your notes.

Note-Taking Styles

There is no "right way" to take notes—you can choose from many note-taking formats. If you're a linear thinker or a list person, you might prefer to take notes straight down a page. If you're a visual learner, you might want to add charts or visual representations to your notes as the instructor speaks. Whatever note-taking style you use, remember to write down your reactions, analysis, and questions. If you add this layer of personal reflection and evaluation to your notes, you will listen more critically to the lecture and will take more thoughtful notes.

Instructor Notes

Your instructor might provide a handout (usually in the form of an outline) as an overview of the class or as a framework for your note-taking. Use this document to guide the way you take notes in class. Either on the handout or in a separate document, take additional notes in your own words. These notes will add more detail to whatever the instructor has already included on the handout. And be sure to write down your personal reaction, analysis, and questions as well.

Your Personal Style of Note-Taking

It's important to take notes that work for you, so feel free to add your personal touch. You can combine the formats described in this chapter, depending on the information being presented and your learning style. For example, to aid your understanding, you might add visual notes to your outline, or combine a table of notes with diagrams.

You might use different note-taking styles in different classes. For example, you might prefer to make graphical representations of theories in your economics class; but in your psychology lectures, you might prefer to take notes in an outline format. Whatever the case, the more you personalize your notes and make them your

PENCIL AND PAPER?! TALK ABOUT *OLD SCHOOL!*

Notes are useful only if they are in a style and format that work for you. Don't worry about what your neighbor is doing, unless you think it will help you understand and engage with the material more fully.

own, the more likely they are to aid your understanding and studying, thus improving your academic performance.

Taking notes critically and thoughtfully requires effort, but the payoff is huge. Because this type of note-taking takes concentration and engagement with the material, you'll have a more thorough grasp of the course. In addition, you'll find it easier to complete assignments and study for tests because staying focused during class means that you won't have to relearn everything from scratch.

Visual Walkthrough

Using the Table Format

The table format is easy to use if you are taking notes by hand or on a computer. Simply create a table with three columns: the first column is for class notes, the second column is for your reaction to the class material, and the third column is for questions you have during class.

Vietnam War : On the Home Front		
Class notes ①	Reaction/ Analysis ②	Questions ③
<u>Mass movements against the war</u> *Students for a Democratic Society (SDS)—Recruited 20,000 people; first major demonstration in DC; SDS chapters in more than 300 college campuses; protests against ROTC, CIA, military research projects, manufacturers of war material *Martin Luther King Jr.— Rebuked US government as "the greatest purveyor of violence in the world today" *Environmentalists—Disgusted by use of chemical weapons (e.g. Agent Orange)	Mass movements were necessary to get President's attention (unfortunate it had to get to this level).	Where did the SDS movement start, and how long did it take to spread to so many campuses?
<u>Antiwar sentiment</u> *Media questioned war—New York Times (1965), Wall Street Journal & Life magazine (by 1968), Walter Cronkite *Prominent Democratic senators urged negotiation instead of force—J. William Fulbright, George McGovern, Mike Mansfield *Women Strike for Peace (WSP)—Founded 1961; working for nuclear disarmament; alerted public to horror & danger of the war)	Important that media took a stand, given media influence in US—must have made a real impact— find out more.	Want to know more about Senate's role in de-escalation of the war— Republicans vs. Democrats?

① The first column is for notes that focus on the substance of what the instructor is saying. You might quote the instructor directly, but usually you'll write short-hand notes in your own words that highlight the important points the instructor is presenting, including concepts, theories, facts, principles, arguments, examples, evidence, and anecdotes.

② The second column is for your personal reaction, analysis, and opinions about the class material. This section is important because it adds a layer of critical thinking to your notes. You might want to use the critical thinking steps outlined in Chapter 4 as a guide for what you should be thinking about during class (for example, whether you agree or disagree with what's being said; whether any information is missing; how your life experiences influence and inform your response to the lecture).

③ The third column is for any questions you have during class. For example, if you don't understand a theory the instructor presents, highlight it in your notes so that you remember to discuss it with the instructor during office hours.

Visual Walkthrough ▶

Using the Outline Format

The outline format is an outline of the details presented during class, including important concepts, theories, facts, principles, arguments, examples, evidence, and anecdotes. This format is helpful for material that is highly structured, although you can use it for any class if you prefer outlining as a way of organizing information. Include your personal reactions, analysis, and questions in your notes — preferably in the margins, to keep your outline clear and concise.

Vietnam War: On the Home Front ①	
Mass movements were necessary to get president's attention (unfortunate it had to get to this level). ⑤ Where did the SDS movement start, and how long did it take to spread to so many campuses?	I. Mass movements against the war ② ③ a. Students for a Democratic Society (SDS) i. Recruited 20,000 people ii. Firstlst major demonstration in ④ DC iii. SDS chapters in more than 300 college campuses iv. Protests against ROTC, CIA, military research projects, manufacturers of war material b. Martin Luther King Jr. i. Rebuked US government as "the greatest purveyor of violence in the world today" c. Environmentalists i. Disgusted by use of chemical weapons (e.g., Agent Orange)
Important that media took a stand, given media influence in US—must have made a real impact—find out more. Want to know more about Senate's role in de-escalation of the war—Republicans vs. Democrats?	II. Antiwar sentiment a. Media questioned war i. New York Times in 1965 ii. Wall Street Journal by 1968 iii. Life magazine by 1968 iv. Walter Cronkite b. Prominent Democratic senators urged negotiation instead of force i. J. William Fulbright ii. George McGovern iii. Mike Mansfield c. Women Strike for Peace (WSP) i. Founded 1961 ii. Worked for nuclear disarmament iii. Alerted public to horror and danger of the war

① This example provides a rough sketch of how you might use an outline to organize information presented during a history class focused on the Vietnam War.

② The main topic—"On the Home Front"—is broken down into major topics (I. and II.).

③ Subtopics (a, b, c, etc.) help clarify the information in the main topic.

④ Relevant details (i, ii, iii, etc.) expand on the subtopics.

⑤ In the margins, add any reactions, analysis, or questions you might have.

Visual Walkthrough

Adding Visuals

You can make your notes more visual in a number of ways: Draw simple diagrams with circles and arrows that connect material. Create flowcharts to visualize information, especially if the material has a natural sequence or flow. Or use an information map, in which key concepts appear in the center of the map and notes radiate from those key points.

The following examples transform aspects of the outlined notes into visual formats.

Diagram

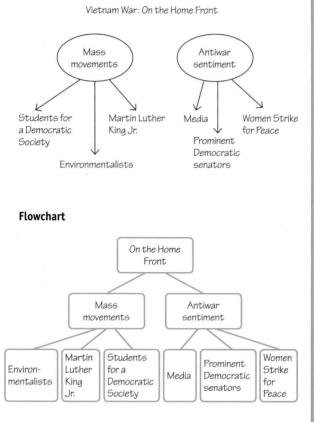

Flowchart

Q **CASE STUDY**

Lucas shares his note-taking preferences.

I figured out that the most effective way I take notes is to use an outline format with headings followed by bullet points. Most of the time, this system works well, but it definitely depends on the class. For example, in classes such as biology, I had to learn more visually, so drawing diagrams really helped my learning. I also recognized that taking notes is especially important when I'm trying to put the "puzzle" of the class together. Because I can constantly refer back to my notes, I'm better able to see how the class topics connect and to tie readings to material the instructor has explained.

QUESTION FOR REFLECTION: If you're using the same note-taking style for each of your classes, would trying a different note-taking style in any of your classes help you understand the material better?

Review Your Notes Early and Often

Most college students leave a class and don't think about it again until it's time to study for a test, complete an assignment, or visit an instructor during office hours. But you can improve your critical thinking and retention of class material by taking ten minutes later in the day to read over your notes. This strategy is an effective way to synthesize what was said during the lecture and to begin to imprint the material on your brain.

QUICK TIP

Quiz Yourself

In addition to reading over your notes, ask yourself
questions about the class to check your retention and
understanding of the material. For example, can you
articulate the key concepts or theories in your own
words? Do you remember an example that was given,
and can you explain it clearly? Were you persuaded by
the evidence provided? If so, why? When you ask
questions, you're finding out what you really know, as
well as reviewing the material in a meaningful way.

Another reason to look over your notes after class is
to figure out what questions you have. Some of your
questions might merely be ponderings that you can
investigate using class readings or while doing outside
research. But other questions might indicate that you're
having difficulty understanding the material; if so, be
sure to ask your instructor or a teaching assistant to
answer them. Either way, it's better to get answers to your
questions early on, rather than having unanswered
questions the night before an exam.

QUICK TIP

Make Connections

Connect your notes to assigned readings. Notes provide
a bridge between what you're learning in class and
what you're reading outside of class. If you don't
understand why your instructor assigned a particular
reading, consult your lecture notes. Thoughtful notes
should help you determine how the lectures relate to
the readings and vice versa.

A final note-taking suggestion: take a few minutes
before class starts to read over your notes from the last
lecture. This strategy will help you remember where the

discussion left off and will help you make connections between different class topics and readings. It will focus your mind on the current class, rather than the class you had earlier in the day. This strategy also provides a few more moments of critical thinking as you assess the big picture of the course, giving you more time to make connections and highlight important details in your mind.

✓ CHECKLIST FOR EFFECTIVE NOTE-TAKING

- ☐ Find a location in class that helps keep you engaged.
- ☐ Practice techniques that increase your focus— turn off devices that may be distracting, breathe deeply, eat a snack.
- ☐ Take notes on the instructor's arguments, evidence, examples, theories, facts, and anecdotes.
- ☐ Take notes on your personal reactions, analysis, and questions along the way.
- ☐ Read over your notes after class and add anything salient.
- ☐ Get answers to any questions you have after reviewing your notes.

Chapter 6
Reading Effectively

The amount of reading assigned in college can be extensive and may come as a surprise. And college reading is often denser than the reading you did in high school. It's normal if you find your reading assignments overwhelming. Sometimes the sheer number of pages you need to get through is the challenge; at other times, the complexity of what you are reading poses difficulty. Whatever the case, you can take certain steps to help you manage it all.

Set Yourself Up for Success

With any assignment in college, your mind-set matters because it will influence the level of concentration and focus you're able to give. With college-level reading in particular, you need a certain level of engagement with the material; otherwise, the reading exercise is a waste of time. It's easy to read words on a page, but if you finish and realize you have no idea what you've been reading, you're not in the right frame of mind.

Location Matters

You can help yourself by finding a location that improves your focus. If you always fall asleep while reading in bed, it's best to find another place to read. Through trial and error, you might determine that a special spot in the student center, with the constant hustle and bustle as background noise, keeps you focused. Or maybe dead silence in the library is what you need.

Break Down Readings

Extensive college reading assignments can feel over-whelming. A simple yet effective strategy to make readings more manageable is to break them down into chunks over the course of one day or even a few days. It's much easier to envision yourself finishing twenty-five pages of reading rather than plowing through a hundred pages. And if you read smaller segments, you'll find it easier to check your understanding of the reading.

Take Steps to Help Yourself

If you stop after doing some reading and find that you haven't retained much, it won't help to continue. Figure out why you might be having trouble and take steps to help yourself. If you're distracted, find another location or read later in the day. If the text is too challenging for you, meet with classmates or an instructor to get some help.

"This is a 'text book', it's a bit like a website but printed on paper."

We're so used to constantly using our electronic devices that college textbooks might feel a bit foreign. Just remember to break down long readings into smaller chunks to make them more manageable.

Remember Time Management

If possible, read when you're most alert. Use your planner to detail when and where you plan to complete your reading assignments each day. Also use a daily to-do list (see Chapter 2) to help you divide your readings into manageable chunks. For example, you might split your reading into three twenty-five-page segments that you plan to finish at three different points over the course of two days. Recognize when it takes you longer than expected to get through a reading so that you can adjust the amount of time you'll need to set aside for similar types of reading assignments in the future.

Read Effectively

Once you're ready to dive into your college readings, it's not enough to read the words and move along. Reading effectively means actually retaining the material. This will help when you need to recall details during class discussions and when you study for tests. The type and length of college reading will vary by subject and class, but you can apply effective reading strategies to any assignment.

Before starting a reading, look through the text, noting aspects that catch your eye, such as highlighted text, images, diagrams, section titles, and summary sections. Scanning the text makes you more familiar with the material before you start reading, and can aid your understanding since your brain has already begun processing aspects of the information presented. Moreover, these text markers often point to essential information that you'll need to remember.

Engage with Your Reading

Engage with your readings as a critical thinker. You will read more effectively if you apply the five steps for critical thinking outlined in Chapter 4.

Step 1: Ask questions frequently. Before you begin to read, ask where the reading fits into the course as a whole (to provide context for the material). While reading the text, check your understanding by periodically pausing and asking yourself questions: Is this an important detail? Can I fully picture the example provided? What evidence supports the argument? Do I remember the theory I just read?

Step 2: React as you read. Evaluate the text as you read, checking whether it makes sense, and gauge your opinion of the arguments presented, the examples given, and the effectiveness of the author's writing. If you're reading a scientific piece, examine the experimental procedure and statistics to be sure they are sound.

Step 3: Ask what's missing. Critically analyze the information presented to decide if anything—such as evidence or other perspectives—might be missing. This step will also help you think about whether the information is biased in a particular direction. For example, if other viewpoints and examples had been included, would you view the text differently?

Step 4: Think about the big picture. As you read, make connections between different parts of the text. Then, take it a step further by making connections to other class readings, lectures, and assignments. How does the reading speak to other aspects of the class?

Step 5: Personalize the text. While reading, check if your personal experiences inform your understanding of the material. As you're reading, what matters to you? Why does it matter to you? How do your experiences help you understand and interpret the reading in a unique way?

✓ CRITICAL READING CHECKLIST

- ☐ Ask questions frequently while you read.
- ☐ Evaluate the text while you read.
- ☐ Ask yourself what's missing from the text.
- ☐ Consider the big picture and connect the reading to other aspects of the class.
- ☐ Personalize the text whenever possible.

These critical thinking steps are intended to guide your thinking while you read. Some of the steps might be more relevant than others, depending on the reading assignment. But with practice, they will become a natural part of your reading process.

Take Notes

To fully engage yourself while reading, take critical thinking notes along the way. Write down your questions and reactions, take note if you think a perspective is missing, outline your synthesis clearly, and don't forget to personalize the text. You might decide to take notes in the margins of the reading, on a separate piece of paper, or on a computer.

Use symbols. Using symbols while you take notes on a reading can help your reading process. For example, you might use an exclamation point to represent your agreement; draw a circle around examples; add a question mark if you don't understand something or if you find some evidence questionable; and use arrows to indicate aspects of the text that connect in some way.

Use a highlighter sparingly. Students often use high-lighters to call out important aspects of the text. However, if you highlight too much of the text, the highlighting becomes useless because you end up having to reread most of the material anyway. Moreover, indiscriminate highlighting reduces critical thinking because you're not pausing to ask questions and react meaningfully. If you love highlighters, give your high-lighting a specific and limited purpose.

Take extra time to save yourself time. Although taking notes increases the amount of time you need to get through a reading, the positive trade-off is that your comprehension and engagement with the reading will be much greater. As a result, you'll retain more of the material in the short and long term. You will find it easier to complete assignments that require use of the reading. And studying the reading for tests won't take as long because you can just study your notes, rather than rereading the entire text.

Visual Walkthrough

Take Critical Thinking Notes While You Read

Taking notes that push you to think critically while you read will help you better understand and retain the text. Moreover, you'll be able to refer back to your reading notes when you study for tests or if you need to use the text for assignments or projects.

The Internationalization of the United States

① Globalization was typically associated with the expansion of American enterprise and culture to other countries, yet the United States experienced the dynamic forces of globalization within its own borders. Already in the 1980s, Japanese, European, and Middle Eastern investors had purchased American stocks and bonds, real estate, and corporations such as Firestone and 20th Century Fox. Local communities welcomed foreign capital, and states competed to recruit foreign automobile plants. American non-union workers began to produce Hondas in Marysville, Ohio, and BMWs in Spartanburg, South Carolina. By 2002, the paychecks of nearly four million American workers came from foreign-owned companies. ??? But were American workers also laid off?

② *Foreigner investing & purchase in the U.S.*

⑤ *!!!* Globalization was transforming not just the economy but American society as well, as the United States experienced a tremendous surge of immigration, part of a worldwide trend that counted some 214 million immigrants across the globe in 2010. By 2006, the United States' 35.7 million immigrants constituted 12.4 percent of the population. The 20 million who arrived between 1980 and 2005 surpassed the previous peak immigration of the first two decades of the twentieth century and exhibited a striking difference in country of origin. Eighty-five percent of the earlier immigrants had come from Europe; by the 1980s, the vast majority came from Asia and Latin America. Consequently, immigration changed the racial and ethnic composition of the nation. By 2004, Asian Americans numbered 13 million, while 41 million Latinos constituted — at 14 percent — the largest minority group in the nation.

⑥ [highlighted]

③ [circled]

④ [circled] ??? But didn't this "promise" work out for most?

The promise of economic opportunity, as always, lured immigrants to America, and the Immigration and Nationality Act of 1965 enabled them to come. Although the law set an annual limit of 270,000 immigrants, it allowed close relatives of U.S. citizens to enter above the ceiling, thus creating family migration chains. In addition, the Cold War dispersal of U.S. military and other personnel around the world enabled foreigners to learn about the nation and form relationships with citizens. Moreover, during the Cold War, U.S. immigration policy was generous to refugees from communism, welcoming more than 800,000 Cubans after Castro's revolution in 1959 and more than 600,000 Vietnamese, Laotians, and Cambodians after the Vietnam War.

⑦ *Families from home benefitted*

---

① Underline main ideas and key concepts.

② Take summarizing notes in the margins.

③ Circle specific examples.

④ Use question marks when you have a question or don't understand something in the text.

⑤ Use exclamation marks to indicate agreement.

⑥ Use a highlighter for one purpose — maybe to highlight important dates or numbers.

⑦ Personalize the text whenever you can.

**⑤ QUESTIONS TO ANSWER AFTER
   COMPLETING A READING**

1. **What are the most important themes or
    concepts?**

    This will help you assess whether you understood the
    essence of the reading. And if you don't know, you need
    to go back and find out.

2. **What examples or significant details should I
    remember?**

    Dig deeper into the material so that you can round out
    the overarching themes and concepts with supporting
    details.

3. **Is the evidence presented sound? Why or why
    not?**

    Take a step back and analyze the evidence presented to
    push yourself to engage in critical thinking that will
    increase your deep understanding.

4. **Does the material contradict or support other
    readings or lectures? How?**

    Connect the reading to others in the class and to what
    was argued in lecture to help pick out broader course
    themes and main arguments.

5. **Why did the instructor assign the piece of
    reading? What's the point of the reading?**

    Asking why the material is important in the scheme of
    the course will help you determine what aspects of the
    reading matter most.

Engage in Conversations

Another way to improve the effectiveness and comprehension of your reading is to talk about the material. As
you talk about how various readings have shaped your
understanding, you'll engage your brain in critical
thinking, figure out what you know and don't know, and
learn from other perspectives.

Get Support from Classmates

Form a reading group or find a classmate who is interested
in working with you, and share your questions, reactions,
and synthesis of assigned texts. As a time saver, meet once
a week over lunch or dinner. Engaging with the texts by

discussing them with other students will benefit you because you'll be more likely to notice if you don't fully understand something in the readings. And you may be forced to rethink your understanding of the texts, helping to deepen your comprehension.

Review Your Reading

If you find yourself lost during a reading group discussion, go back to the text to make sure you're not missing anything important. And if this happens frequently, it could be a sign that you need extra help in the class. Visit the Academic Advising Office to talk with an advisor about your struggles, or find a tutor who can meet with you regularly.

Meet with Instructors and Teaching Assistants

It's also useful to talk with your instructor or teaching assistant about readings. Visit during office hours or spend a few minutes after class explaining what you find fascinating or what doesn't seem to make sense. Find out why your instructor assigned the reading and whether he or she can help you make deeper connections with other class material. These discussions will further your critical thinking in meaningful ways.

If you're having trouble understanding the readings, be sure to meet with your instructor. Giving your instructor a sense of the challenges you are facing in the class will allow him or her to provide more focused assistance. And if you find that you can't get through all the readings or can't stay focused while reading, be honest about this. Your instructor might provide you with course-specific reading techniques or may refer you to the Academic Advising Office for assistance.

Q CASE STUDY

Ken explains how he deals with college reading assignments.

With so many assigned readings, it can be tough to prioritize. I found that the best way to stay on top of all the readings is to plan ahead. The biggest difficulty I had was time management. During my first year, I would start my readings after dinner, which would usually lead to a late night. I was very motivated and eager to get straight A's, so often I would stay up until 2 a.m. or even later. I thought this is how hard you're supposed to work in college to succeed, but I could have simply worked smarter and attended class without feeling exhausted.

During my second year, I broke my study sessions into blocks throughout the day. I read while riding a stationary bike at the gym or while I was at work. I did my readings anywhere I had the opportunity in order to reduce the workload later. When nighttime came around, I didn't look at my readings as a never-ending task because I had already finished most of it during the day.

Another great benefit that came with this new habit was that I was better able to retain the information I read. When I did all my readings in one segment for several hours straight, I found that I couldn't recall the information as clearly as when I had breaks between my readings. Taking breaks helps retention because the brain can absorb only so much information before it runs out of energy. Spreading my readings throughout the day was one of the most important changes I made in college.

QUESTIONS FOR REFLECTION: Have you been able to complete readings by the due date, or do you find that you're constantly playing catch-up? If you're struggling to get through your readings, first determine the cause: Are you not giving yourself enough time? Are you distracted while you're reading? Or are you having trouble understanding the texts? Then, try a new reading strategy to address the issue: for example, start readings at least three days before the due date; change your reading location; write more notes using critical thinking strategies; or seek help from your instructor and the Academic Advising Office.

OFFICE
HOURS

You may have studied a lot, a little, or not at all in high school. In college, though, studying is an important part of life. Exams are usually less frequent in college than in high school, so the amount of material covered in college exams is much greater. To retain all the information you need to remember when you take a test, you need different study habits than you did in high school. Knowing how to study in college is a skill that you can master through planning, connecting, conversations, and practice.

Move beyond Memorization

Although you have to memorize some material, studying solely by memorizing information won't be effective in college. College tests require a deeper understanding of the material—an understanding that asks you to apply theories or facts to novel problems and questions, or to make connections and draw conclusions that may not be obvious.

First-year students are sometimes baffled when they receive exam grades that are lower than they expected, especially if they studied hard and believed they fully understood the material. Often, though, they merely memorized the material and lacked the deep understanding that instructors expect.

Let's look at some examples.

- In college, it's not enough to memorize the definition of a principle in economics. Instructors expect you to have a deeper understanding of the principle and will ask you to apply the principle to problems you've never seen or talked about before.

- If you're taking a human anatomy class, you'll need to do more than memorize the functions of the different parts of the body. College instructors expect you to know how the parts are connected to one another and how they interact.

- In a history class covering the civil rights movement, a test question might ask you to discuss what impact the movement had on the presidential campaigns of the 1960s and 1970s. To answer this question, you need an in-depth understanding of how events of the period influenced politics, political party dynamics, race relations, and much more. Just memorizing facts and dates won't help you answer this question. You have to think critically and be able to analyze the connections between events.

Start with Time Management

To make the most of your study sessions, use the time management tools discussed in Chapter 2.

Set a start date. Once you receive a class syllabus, use your planner to establish your study schedule for all exams and tests. Plan to begin studying at least three to five days before a test to be sure that you have enough time to cover all the material and to ask questions if you don't understand something. If you give yourself some extra time for studying, you're prepared in case the unexpected happens—for example, if an assignment for another class takes longer than you expected or if you get sick. By building in a few extra days for your studying, you won't have to stay up all night cramming the day before a test.

Determine time and location. If you study at a time when you focus best, you're likely to do more than memorize. And location matters, too. Try to find a spot that minimizes distractions and maximizes your concentration. Once you've determined your ideal study time and location, add this information to your daily to-do list.

Create a Study Plan

If you take five or ten minutes to develop a study plan, studying for tests will feel less overwhelming. First, make a list of what you need to study, such as lecture notes, readings, problem sets, and assignments. Determine

I REALLY CRAMMED LAST NIGHT.

Although cramming for tests the night before may seem like a good study strategy, it doesn't give your brain enough time to fully retain the material. Try studying over the course of a few days to make sure that you completely understand the information and have time to ask questions, instead of overloading your brain with last-minute studying.

which topics or materials you *don't* need to study. If you're not sure what to study, talk to your instructor or classmates to get help.

Prioritize your list so that you know where to start and how to keep yourself moving through the material. How you prioritize your list depends on your preferences. For example, you might decide that you'd like to study all your lecture notes and then all your readings. Or you might mix it up a bit for variety. It can be helpful to study lecture notes and readings that are connected or on the same topic so that you can determine how the information from various sources is related.

QUICK TIP

Study Difficult Material First

If you are struggling with certain concepts, theories, or readings, study those first. Why? Your brain is usually at its best when you start studying, and it may take you more time to fully understand this type of material. And if you still have trouble understanding the material, you'll have time to get extra help before the test.

Make Connections with Study Notes

With a study plan in place, it's now time to start studying. Some students will reread or scan readings and lecture notes, look over problem sets and assignments, and memorize important concepts. After covering the material in this way, they may feel that they know the material well enough. But usually this type of studying leaves students with a surface knowledge that may not be enough to do well on tests.

To develop a deeper understanding that allows you to successfully tackle test problems you've never seen before or to discuss information in novel ways on exams, take *study notes* that highlight important connections. Study notes will engage your brain more fully because you're not just rereading or skimming; instead, you are meaningfully writing and thinking about the material. Your study notes will facilitate critical thinking if you keep the following ideas in mind.

Create meaningful chunks. Can you group information into meaningful categories or sort it into contrasting categories? The more you pull information into coherent chunks, the more connections your brain is making, thus making it easier to recall the information on tests.

Use visual representations. The more ways you can examine the material you're studying, the more likely

Visual Walkthrough

Outline a Study Plan

A study plan will help you stay organized and focused during your study sessions. If you follow a study plan, you'll be more likely to cover all necessary material and can concentrate on the concepts and readings that are more challenging or confusing. Your study plan also helps you break down material into smaller chunks, making studying more manageable.

STUDY PLAN FOR BIOLOGY 101 TEST			
TOPIC ❶	**MATERIAL TO STUDY** ❷	**CHALLENGING/ CONFUSING?** ❸	**PRIORITY** ❹
Cell biology	Lecture 2–4 notes	Yes	5
	Textbook chapters 4–6	No	8
	3 Journal of Cellular Biology articles	Yes	6
	Lab write-up	No	7
❺ Genetics	Lecture 5–6 notes	Yes	1
	Textbook chapters 9–10	Yes	3
	2 genetics articles from the New England Journal of Medicine	Yes	4
	Lab write-up	Yes	2
Evolution	Lecture 7–8 notes	No	9
	Textbook chapters 11–12	No	10
	On the Origin of Species (Darwin)	No	11

1. This study plan is organized by topic so that all the material within a given topic will be studied as a group. You can use other ways to organize a study plan. For example, you might focus on similar types of material, first studying all lecture notes and then moving on to readings. The choice is yours.

2. The material to study will vary by class, and your plan can be as detailed or as brief as you'd like. However, be specific so that you know exactly what you're supposed to be studying and don't waste valuable time trying to figure out what you meant by "journal articles" or "textbook readings."

3. Determine if the material you'll be studying is particularly challenging or confusing for you.

4. Prioritize your list so you know what to study first, second, third, and so on. Prioritizing will save you time because you'll have an organized plan that keeps you moving in a specified order during your study sessions. Try starting with the more difficult material so that you have enough time to understand it and to ask questions if necessary.

5. Given that all material under the topic of genetics is marked as "challenging/confusing," it's best to start the study session with this material.

you are to understand and remember it. Creating diagrams, charts, graphs, or pictures of information that visually connect details will help you view the material in a new way, improving your retention.

Connect material to your life. In your study notes, try to make connections to your own life by considering how personal experiences affect your reaction to and understanding of the material. This step may sound irrelevant when you are studying, but you'll remember information more easily if it matters to you. And if a test question asks for your opinion on an issue, you will have already developed your own perspective.

> **✓ CHECKLIST OF SUCCESSFUL STUDY STRATEGIES**
>
> ☐ Avoid soft, flat surfaces when studying.
> ☐ Study what you don't know first.
> ☐ Put study notes in your own words as much as possible.
> ☐ Fit a reasonable amount of sleep into your study plan.
> ☐ Study over a period of time to minimize cramming.

Talk about Your Learning

Conversations are a great way to determine what you really know (and what you don't know!). In your planner, be sure to set aside study time with others. You might be someone who prefers to study alone in the quietest corner of the library—this is fine, especially when you're developing a study plan and creating study notes. But if you want to develop a deep understanding of the material, you need to test your understanding out loud.

Study with Others

Form a study group with the goal of helping each other grasp important concepts. And be thoughtful about how many other students you want to include in the group. Sometimes studying with just one other person is enough to test your understanding of the material. Too many voices can make it difficult for any one person to engage in a meaningful dialogue.

Come prepared. Make the most of your study sessions by figuring out beforehand what you want to cover during the study group meeting. You might choose to focus on a particular topic, concept, theory, or reading, or on material you are having difficulty understanding.

Don't waste time during the study session itself trying to figure out what you want to study.

Ask questions and debate. Answering questions will reveal how well you know the material you're studying. If you have trouble responding to a question, you'll know which material you need to revisit before the test. And engaging in a debate will force you to think deeply about the material, especially if you're trying to form arguments and responses on the spot. College tests require that you think on your feet, and practicing in a study group will improve your performance.

Practice individually, then discuss. Bring practice problems and questions to the study group session. First work on them individually; then talk about your answers as a group. This technique can highlight what each member does and doesn't know and can also reveal different perspectives or approaches.

QUICK TIP

Collaborate Virtually
A virtual study group that "meets" through a technology platform can be just as effective as talking in person. Keep this possibility in mind if it means you'll make the time to engage with others on the material you're studying.

Talk to Instructors and Teaching Assistants

Another way to deepen your understanding is to talk with instructors and teaching assistants about what you're studying. Plan ahead to figure out whether you can visit during office hours or at another time. And try to do some individual studying before your meeting so that you can ask clarifying questions and come prepared with topics that are specific and targeted.

Setting up conversations with peers and instructors does take time and effort. You also might feel intimidated in one or both settings if you don't feel confident with the material or if you tend to be shy about sharing your knowledge and thoughts. But these discussions will build your confidence and will make you even more comfortable with the material. Even one conversation could improve your performance on tests by shedding light on what you need to study more deeply.

Q CASE STUDY

Brian shares his perspective on studying.

The question I always ask myself is "What is the purpose of this class, and how does it relate to the environment around me?" Once I figure that out, then it's actually fun to study for exams. The difference between college and high school is that in high school I was studying to get an A in the class. In college, I study to understand and use the information in some aspect of my life. An educator I admire said that if students can chase after knowledge instead of degrees, they will have a more meaningful experience in their classes. This is the mentality that drives my actions when it comes to studying and taking exams.

When studying, I practice an exercise called "once you teach it, you know it." I attempt to engage in some form of conversation with a peer about the topic at hand and try to further my knowledge by making it as practical as possible.

QUESTIONS FOR REFLECTION: Have you formed a study group to help you study for tests? If so, has it been helpful? Do you find that you're able to stay on task, or do you often waste time? If you're not using your time together effectively, be honest with yourself and your study group, and determine what you can do to make your study time together more productive.

Practice Tests Are Key

An essential study tip is to practice, practice, practice. The results of a practice test will reveal which topics or concepts you don't know well enough. You'll also find out if you're struggling to recall information fast enough to complete the test in the time allotted. Taking practice tests will help your performance on actual tests.

Ask for Old Exams

Your instructor might be happy to share past exams, especially if you tell him or her that you plan to use the exams as a study tool. If not, then talk to the instructor about the test format (the number of questions and the types of questions) so that you can put together your own practice tests.

Create Your Own Practice Tests

If you can't get your hands on an old exam, then put together a practice test using old assignments or quizzes you've already taken in the class. For example, in an engineering class, take old problem sets and use those as your practice tests, but be sure to hide the answers so that you're truly testing your knowledge.

Time Practice Tests Appropriately

Be sure to take practice tests within a limited time frame. If you give yourself an unlimited amount of time, you may not work fast enough on the actual exam. And sometimes the timed nature of tests is what causes anxiety. It's easy to get stuck on a problem and find it difficult to move on. However, if you learn to push yourself through a practice test, you'll find it easier to complete the actual test in the allotted time.

Build in time for practice tests in your study plan. And once you've taken a practice test, go back and check your answers, paying close attention to what you got wrong, what you struggled to answer, and what you couldn't answer. Grading your practice test will provide a road map for the topics and concepts you need to study more thoroughly before the actual test. You'll also determine what questions still remain so that you can get some help from classmates, your instructor, or a teaching assistant.

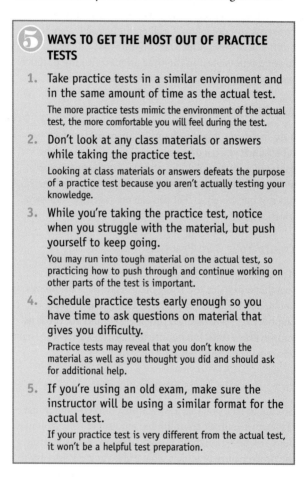

WAYS TO GET THE MOST OUT OF PRACTICE TESTS

1. **Take practice tests in a similar environment and in the same amount of time as the actual test.**

   The more practice tests mimic the environment of the actual test, the more comfortable you will feel during the test.

2. **Don't look at any class materials or answers while taking the practice test.**

   Looking at class materials or answers defeats the purpose of a practice test because you aren't actually testing your knowledge.

3. **While you're taking the practice test, notice when you struggle with the material, but push yourself to keep going.**

   You may run into tough material on the actual test, so practicing how to push through and continue working on other parts of the test is important.

4. **Schedule practice tests early enough so you have time to ask questions on material that gives you difficulty.**

   Practice tests may reveal that you don't know the material as well as you thought you did and should ask for additional help.

5. **If you're using an old exam, make sure the instructor will be using a similar format for the actual test.**

   If your practice test is very different from the actual test, it won't be a helpful test preparation.

QUICK TIP

Practice Makes Perfect

As the saying goes, "Practice makes perfect." If possible, try to fit in more than one practice test in your study plan. The more you test your knowledge, the more likely you'll be able to perform at your peak during the actual test.

Test-Taking

Your first big college exam is tomorrow. You have a good grasp of the material, but you'd like to study additional readings and class notes. Should you plan to stay up really late to finish studying? Should you also study right before the start of the exam instead of eating breakfast? Perhaps you're feeling anxious and hope you don't blank during the test, which has happened to you in the past. And what if you don't finish the exam in time? This chapter addresses test-taking questions you might have and offers advice to help you perform at your best.

Before the Test

One of the most important things you can do before a test is to study well in advance (see Chapter 7). Plan ahead by starting your studying at least a few days, if not a few weeks, before the test to give yourself time to take thoughtful study notes and to ask any pressing questions. Studying in advance will help you digest the material more fully and will reduce anxiety because you won't be trying to cram every little detail into your brain the night before.

Cramming typically doesn't work for college tests because it leaves you with only a surface-level understanding, rather than a deep grasp of the material. When you give your brain just a limited amount of time to learn the information, you're more likely to forget what you studied. You may also have a harder time recalling details and applying what you know to novel problems that are on the exam.

The Night Before

Try to get a good night's sleep before the test. A good night's sleep varies from person to person, but most people need a six- to eight-hour block of sleep. When you're tired, your brain doesn't function as well as it does when you're rested. Lack of sleep makes it more difficult for you to remember things and to be creative, and your ability to recall information slows down—factors that can negatively affect your performance on tests.

So, the night before an exam, determine when you'd like to go to bed, and add that to your study plan. If you want to get a reasonable amount of sleep, you may have to modify your study plan so that you study only the most important material (instead of everything you had hoped to cover). And remember, you may be able to move some of your studying to the next morning, depending on when the test is scheduled. Knowing that you'll have some time the next day to continue your studying could be a good incentive to get yourself to bed.

The Morning of the Test

If you plan to finish studying the morning of the test, be careful not to cram in too much. A rushed morning will only increase your stress. Give yourself enough time to get ready, and be sure to dress in something that makes you feel comfortable—the last thing you should be thinking about is how uncomfortable you are while taking the test. If you're particularly anxious, especially on your way to the test, try using some techniques to calm yourself, such as listening to music or deep breathing.

QUICK TIP

Feed Your Mind

Take time to eat something substantial that will help you maintain your energy and focus. Tests can be quite taxing on your brain, so you need fuel to keep yourself going. And bring a snack and a drink to the test in case you need a boost in the middle of the exam.

Right before the Test

Be sure to get to the test with time to spare. Arriving early means that you'll be able to find a seat that feels comfortable. Maybe you need the extra leg room at the end of a row or prefer to be near a window. Increasing your comfort level during the test will only help you. The additional time will also give you the chance to look over any final materials or your study notes and to begin focusing on the task ahead.

During the Test

There's a lot to think about once you start the exam. Not only are you trying to answer questions correctly, thoroughly, and thoughtfully, but you're also trying to complete the test in the time allotted. Looking over the exam, checking the clock periodically, and keeping yourself focused will help.

Look Over the Exam

As soon as you receive the exam, take a minute to check the number of questions and the amount of time you have to complete it. Then determine how much of the test you need to complete by the halfway mark of the time allotted, and write that on the top of the test. Finally, be sure you understand the directions. It's easy to read directions quickly and misunderstand what you're being asked to do. Having points taken off your score merely for misunderstanding directions can be frustrating, especially if you knew the correct answer.

QUICK TIP

Warm Up before Tests

Before starting to answer questions, some students like to quickly skim the entire test. This technique can help get your brain going as it begins processing the answers to the questions. But be careful. Some students end up feeling more overwhelmed and anxious if they read through the test, especially if many of the questions are particularly challenging. Do what's right for you.

If you have any questions, ask them early in the test. Don't be afraid or embarrassed to do this. If you want to do well on the test, you need to understand what is being asked of you. Sitting and stewing about your confusion only increases your stress. Getting answers to your questions on the test could make all the difference.

Keep Track of Time

Try to pace yourself by checking the clock periodically. It's easy to stay stuck on one problem for a long time, but this wastes valuable time. The longer you mull over a difficult question, the more anxious and frustrated you can become, blocking the free flow of thought and making it even harder to come up with the answer.

Keep moving. If you find yourself getting stuck on a question, circle that question and then move on to the next one. Your subconscious is actually still working on the questions you skip, and you'll likely gain insight as you move to other questions. Just remember to go back to any questions you skipped, to see if you can come up with the answers.

Assess your progress. Once your time is halfway up, assess where you are in the test. If you're about where you should be, keep going. If you're ahead of where you should be, keep going. If you're behind and don't know how you're ever going to answer all the remaining questions, try to shorten your answers if possible, and keep going.

Be concise. Answers to exam questions don't have to be beautifully written. When time is short, you might need to write in shorthand or use bullet points. Write as much as time allows, even if your response is not as thorough as you'd like. If you leave the question blank because time is short, your instructor might assume that you didn't know the answer at all; but if you answer the question, even briefly, your instructor will see that you've grasped aspects of the material.

Visual Walkthrough

Taking the Test

Once the test is handed out, don't immediately start answering the questions. Take a minute to look over the test to get a sense of what you will need to complete in the time allotted.

---

1 Name _____

Psychology 101 Exam (start time 11:00 a.m.)

2 *Directions: Answer the following five short-answer questions in as much detail as possible (each question is worth* **3** *15 points). Then, define the five terms outlined at the end of the exam (each definition is worth 5 points). You have* **4** *one hour to complete the exam. Good luck!*

Short Answer Questions: (Need to finish this section by 11:45 **5** a.m.)

1. What are the five stages of personality development from birth to adolescence, and what defines each of these stages?

2. At what stage does a child's conscience develop, and what influences are important?

3. What are the sources of human self-esteem, according to Sigmund Freud?

4. How has Freud's model of the ego evolved over time, and what does the ego have to control?

5. What constitutes a "healthy" personality in adulthood, according to Marie Jahoda?

Define the following terms: (Spend no more than 3 minutes **5** on each term.)

a. Epigenetic principle

b. Incorporative stage

c. Precocious conscience

d. Identity confusion

e. Distantiation

1. Be sure to write your name on the test.

2. Read the directions carefully to be sure you know what is expected. Then, quickly skim each page of the test to familiarize yourself with what's to come.

3. Calculate how much of the total grade each question represents. The first five short-answer questions are worth 75 percent of the grade, while the five definitions are worth 25 percent. Spend more time on those questions that are worth more, so try to allocate your time accordingly: you should spend about 75 percent of your time (45 minutes) on the first five questions, and the remainder of your time (15 minutes) on the definitions.

4. Note how much time you have to complete the exam so that you can figure out where you should be at specific points in the test. Since the time allotted is one hour and the start time is 11 a.m., you need to complete the five short-answer questions by 11:45 a.m. to give yourself enough time to define the five terms at the end of the test. Check the clock periodically. If you're still on question 2 at the halfway point (11:30 a.m.), you'll need to move more quickly through the remaining questions to complete the test in time.

5. Write notes on the exam to help you. For example, write down when you need to complete certain sections or how much time you should spend on specific questions.

Focus on You (Not on Your Classmates!)

Don't compare yourself to those around you during the test. Don't waste your valuable time and brainpower worrying that your neighbor is already on page 3 of the exam when you're still on page 1. Your neighbor may not have answered all the questions or may have a different strategy for completing the test. Whatever the case, stay focused on you. Check the time, not your peers, to help you move through the test.

QUICK TIP

Check Your Work

If you have time left, go back and look at your answers. Never leave an exam early. Instead, check your answers to be sure you feel confident in them. Add more detail if you can. Sometimes you'll remember something as you're going along and can add information or examples to earlier questions. Be the last one sitting in the exam and not the first one to leave. Checking your work always pays off.

Don't Let Your Eyes Wander—Ever

Be careful not to show any signs of cheating. Keep your eyes focused on the exam or on the clock, not on your neighbor. Cheating is a very serious offense, and if instructors catch you cheating or even suspect you of cheating, you will face severe consequences. You may fail the class, be suspended for a term or a year, or even be expelled from school.

If you feel tempted to cheat, ask yourself why. Are you struggling to understand concepts in the class and don't think you'll pass otherwise? Do you have trouble performing to your capacity on tests and don't know what else to do? Are you not studying enough to do well on the test? No matter what your reasons may be, cheating is dishonest and could severely impact your future and your relationships. Before you resort to cheating, take the time to get tutoring or help with test-taking and studying. You'll be happy you did.

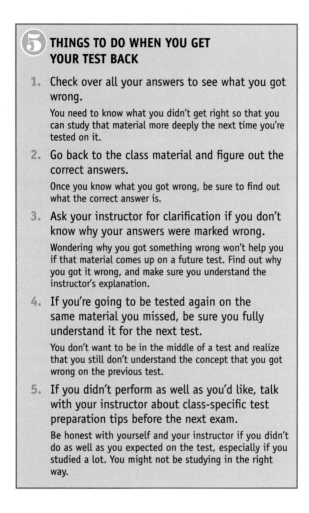

5 THINGS TO DO WHEN YOU GET YOUR TEST BACK

1. Check over all your answers to see what you got wrong.

   You need to know what you didn't get right so that you can study that material more deeply the next time you're tested on it.

2. Go back to the class material and figure out the correct answers.

   Once you know what you got wrong, be sure to find out what the correct answer is.

3. Ask your instructor for clarification if you don't know why your answers were marked wrong.

   Wondering why you got something wrong won't help you if that material comes up on a future test. Find out why you got it wrong, and make sure you understand the instructor's explanation.

4. If you're going to be tested again on the same material you missed, be sure you fully understand it for the next test.

   You don't want to be in the middle of a test and realize that you still don't understand the concept that you got wrong on the previous test.

5. If you didn't perform as well as you'd like, talk with your instructor about class-specific test preparation tips before the next exam.

   Be honest with yourself and your instructor if you didn't do as well as you expected on the test, especially if you studied a lot. You might not be studying in the right way.

Q CASE STUDY

Natasha shares her test-taking advice.

It is important to take advantage of all of your resources. Instructors almost always have office hours available for their students to come in and ask questions before the test, and they can usually be reached through e-mail. A couple of days before the exam, many instructors also set up a review session that is open to their students. It's important to go to those sessions and ask your instructor to clarify any confusing points about the exam or the material.

The night before the test, don't stay up late studying. Sleep and nutrition will be better for you than spending the late hours poring over your books. On test day, get up early and allow yourself time to be comfortable—and be sure to eat a good breakfast.

When you receive the test, flip through it quickly after listening to or reading the directions to make sure you know how to pace yourself. It is important to gauge your time and go back over your work if you have time to spare.

Know what to expect before you arrive at the test. If you know what the exam will look like and have an idea of what type of questions will be asked, you can prepare for it. The good thing is that most instructors will help you out and will let you know what the exams are going to be like! Being proactive is what will help you the most.

QUESTIONS FOR REFLECTION: What has been your experience with test-taking? Have you successfully paced yourself during tests, or do you run out of time and leave questions blank? If you run out of time, reflect on what's happening during the test so that you can find solutions. Are you moving too slowly through the test because you lose track of time or get stuck on questions? Are you dealing with test anxiety? Use the strategies discussed in this chapter to address any test issues you're facing. If you continue to struggle, seek help from the Academic Advising Office.

Managing Test Anxiety

Exams in college can feel quite weighty since they often count for a significant part of your grade. And because just a few tests are given in most college classes, each test score has a big impact on your final grade in the class. Given these factors, it's normal to experience test anxiety. Fortunately, you can use a variety of strategies that reduce this anxiety before and during the exam.

Practice, Practice, Practice

If you play an instrument or play on a sports team, you know that your skill and comfort level improve the more you practice. The same benefits of practice apply to test-taking. The more you practice and put yourself in testing situations, the easier test-taking becomes. So, take practice tests that have the same types of questions as an upcoming test (see Chapter 7), and put yourself in situations that mimic the surroundings and time frame of the test. Becoming more familiar with something puts you at ease — a good starting point before taking an exam.

Reduce Your Stress

Do everything you can to reduce your stress the day of the test. We discussed some of these techniques earlier in the chapter: Arrive at the test early so that you can find a good seat. Wear clothing that makes you feel comfortable. Eat something nutritious that will maintain your energy during the test.

And finally, another key to reducing test anxiety is to avoid classmates who are anxious or overly negative. Your anxiety will only increase if you listen to comments such as "This test is going to be impossible" or "I'm so worried" or "I bet there will be tons of trick questions." Steer clear of these types of negative exchanges before the test.

SNAPSHOTS

College tests usually are less frequent and cover much more material than do tests in high school. But if you want to retain all you need to know, use the study strategies outlined in Chapter 7: plan ahead and study over the course of several days, rather than cramming for the test the night before.

If You Blank

Students sometimes freeze while taking a test. Their hearts start racing, their mind goes blank, and they can't remember the information they need to answer the questions. If you blank, try not to panic. Instead, take steps to calm yourself and alter your state of mind. The strategies in the following checklist will help you regain your composure and get back on track.

> ### ✓ CHECKLIST FOR REDUCING TEST ANXIETY
>
> ☐ **Take several deep breaths.** Continue for a few minutes until you get your breathing and heart rate under control.
>
> ☐ **Tense and then relax different muscle groups.** Move your shoulders in circles, massage your lower back, and move your feet around to get blood flowing.
>
> ☐ **Think of positive images to reduce your anxiety.** Picture a scene you find peaceful, and think about what you see, hear, feel, and smell.
>
> ☐ **Eat or drink something satisfying that will make you feel better.**
>
> ☐ **Use positive self-talk to help you cope and move you forward.** For example, repeat, "I have the ability to do this," *not* "I'm going to fail this test."
>
> ☐ **Think briefly about post-exam rewards.** What fun will you have after the exam is over?

Once you feel calmer, slowly reread the question or problem you're stuck on, and freewrite for a few minutes just to get you going. Write whatever comes into your head. Don't worry about what it sounds like. Just write down what you know. Then, go back and work through as much of the problem as you can, using your freewriting as a guide. Your answer may not be perfect, but giving an imperfect answer is better than leaving the question blank.

And if you still can't answer the question, skip it. Move on to an easier question that you *can* answer. Working on other questions may jog your memory so that later you can go back and answer the questions you skipped.

When to Get Help

Blanking on a test is frightening. Feelings of anxiety can take over, making it difficult to write coherent answers to questions or to complete portions of the test. If you try the techniques discussed in this chapter and they don't help, something more may be going on. For example, you may not be studying in the most effective way. Or stresses in your personal life may be affecting your academic life.

Whatever the case, be sure to seek out help whenever you experience severe test anxiety. Go to your advisor, your instructor, your teaching assistant, your mentor, or someone at the Academic Advising Office, and explain what happens to you when you take a test. One of these people will be able to give you the support you need. Remember: you're never alone in these situations. The more you try to hide your anxiety, the worse it will get. Your college success depends on seeking help when you need it.

Writing and Information Literacy

Writing in college can feel a bit overwhelming, especially during your first year. The expectations of your college instructors will likely be different from those of your high school teachers, and the assignments may be longer and more challenging. But if you plan ahead, incorporate critical thinking, and ask for feedback, you will be able to tackle papers with ease while also improving your writing skills.

General Writing Advice

Don't be surprised if you get lower grades on your first college papers or more constructive criticism than you're used to. Remember that writing is a process and that you can improve your writing with practice. You need to be patient with yourself and be ready to work hard at developing your writing skills. Get a good start by keeping the following three suggestions in mind.

Understand the Assignment

Take the time to fully understand the paper assignment and expectations. Although writing is a personal process, you do have to answer the question that's being asked. Even if you produce a great piece of writing, you won't do well if you don't follow the assignment. Your instructor will grade your paper based on his or her perspective and expectations, so meet with your instructor well in advance of the due date to be sure you're interpreting the assignment properly.

Be honest with your instructor if this is the first time you've encountered a particular type of writing assignment. Ask to see an example of a solid, well-written paper. Find out if your instructor has any course-specific writing strategies or advice to make the process go more smoothly for you. Before you talk with your instructor about the writing assignment, consider how you might approach the topic. The more thinking you do in advance of the meeting, the more clearly you can discuss the assignment and whether you're on the right track. Your instructor might even offer additional insight to help you develop your ideas more fully.

Write Rough Drafts

Plan ahead by writing a rough draft of your paper a few days—or, better yet, a week—before it's due. To craft a well-written paper, you need to write a few drafts before you hand in the final paper. Writing a draft will reduce your paper-writing stress in a couple of ways: it will ease you into writing the final product, and because you're planning ahead, you won't be under extreme time pressure when writing.

Writing papers requires a good deal of thought, so it's an easy task to procrastinate. Help yourself by using your planner to determine when you'll start and finish your draft. Be sure to complete the draft by the deadline you set so that you have time to edit the draft and can ask someone else to provide comments. Editing and feedback will greatly improve your paper.

Obtain Feedback

Someone else should read your paper before you hand it in. Another perspective and a second pair of eyes will help you see where evidence is missing, where your writing is too wordy, where your argument can be fine-tuned, and where your sentences and word choice can be improved.

If you have a writing center on campus, be sure to use it. Taking advantage of this academic resource will ensure that your papers are well developed and that you're getting a fresh and experienced perspective on your writing. Writing tutors and advisors can assist you with all aspects of your paper, including your argument and conclusions, the paper's format and structure, grammar, and so on. To fight paper-writing procrastination, schedule a meeting with a writing center tutor several days or a week before your paper is due to be sure you complete the draft early, get the feedback you need, and have time to make necessary changes for an improved final product.

Visit the Writing Center

Writing center tutors can do more than just read your drafts. They can also help you brainstorm and pick a paper topic, and they are a good sounding board if you can't get started or don't know what else to write.

If you're unable to use a writing center, have others read over your paper draft—your instructor, an advisor, a mentor, or even other students. Any feedback will help you write a stronger paper. Don't hesitate to ask for assistance.

⑤ EASY WAYS TO IMPROVE YOUR PAPERS

1. **Write an introduction that draws your reader in.**

   An introduction sets the scene for the rest of the paper. If it's good, your readers' first impressions will be positive. If it's not good, readers might view the rest of the paper in a more negative light.

2. **Vary sentence length to make the paper more interesting.**

   Too many long sentences can be boring, and too many short sentences can feel choppy. Variety helps keep the reader engaged.

3. **Don't use too many quotations from your sources; instead, interpret your sources in an interesting way.**

   Instructors want to see your critical thinking. So quote sparingly, and spend most of the paper interpreting your sources.

4. **Don't spend the entire conclusion of your essay summarizing your argument; instead, add a novel insight that your reader will remember.**

   Leave the reader with something to think about, rather than a mere summary of the previous pages.

5. **Be sure to edit, edit, edit!**

   Instructors may give you a lower grade on your paper if they find careless errors. So take the time to carefully edit and proofread your paper.

Apply Critical Thinking

Writing papers requires thinking, especially critical thinking. When you're completing writing assignments, be sure to apply the five steps for critical thinking that you learned in Chapter 4. Following these steps will deepen your thinking when you tackle your writing assignments.

Step 1: Ask Questions

Before you begin writing, ask yourself what you need to include in the paper both to answer the question and to meet your instructor's expectations. What topics could you write about, and which ones seem more interesting or more plausible? If you need to incorporate class readings into the paper, which ones are most relevant, and why? If you want to prove an argument, what evidence and examples do you need to provide in order to produce a strong paper? The more questions you ask and answer in advance, the more you're thinking critically about the paper.

Step 2: Evaluate Your Reactions

Evaluate your reactions to the assignment and to your research, and allow these reactions to guide how you will approach the paper. Let's say you need to incorporate two readings into your writing assignment, and you disagree with both authors. Use this reaction to inspire the core of the paper, in which you might thoughtfully present counterarguments to the two authors' arguments.

Or if you're writing a laboratory report for a science class and your results don't conform with the course textbook, you could analyze why you think this is the case. This type of analysis shows that you've thought carefully about the information presented.

Step 3: Write with a "Critical Lens"

Consider how you can incorporate novel insights into your paper. In your readings, have you found any holes in the arguments? Has any evidence been skewed or ignored? In your paper, demonstrate that you have thoughtfully considered several perspectives, and explain why you believe each argument is or is not clearly articulated and supported. This type of thinking will demonstrate that you're not taking everything you're learning at face value; instead, you are critically analyzing material in a meaningful way.

Step 4: Make Connections

By making meaningful connections among disparate aspects of the class in your paper—for example, by exploring how the lectures connect to the readings—you can examine the big picture without losing sight of important details. Synthesizing all the course material could reveal important insights and may push your thinking to a deeper level, improving the paper.

Step 5: Bring Your Experiences into the Assignment

Bringing "you" into your papers may not work in some subjects, but in others it can shape your thinking and make the paper more interesting and meaningful. Let's say you're completing a paper in a political science class and you realize that your involvement in a political campaign offers useful insights. Try to incorporate this experience into your paper—doing so can deepen your argument and help you answer the question in a unique way.

CASE STUDY

Yen shares her thoughts on how to handle college writing assignments.

I found that my most powerful papers happen when I write about what interests me the most. When I get a topic, I like to sleep on it for several nights and let my ideas flow before I sit down to draft an outline. I must immerse myself in the topic in order to write a paper that I truly enjoy. Sometimes it is very tempting for students to complete a paper during a single block of three or four hours. Some students can do well this way.

I realized that the papers I feel most proud of writing are the ones I developed a relationship with—that is, I spent time getting to know everything about the topic, communicating with others (such as a professor or classmates), familiarizing myself with the sources (such as books and peer-reviewed articles), and then forming a final statement about my impression and thoughts. These papers end up being well written, and my grades reflect that, too.

QUESTIONS FOR REFLECTION: What has been your experience so far with writing papers? Do you find it difficult to start writing? If so, how do you get yourself going? If you procrastinate and wait until the last minute, consider making an appointment with the writing center to help motivate you to write a rough draft in advance.

Reduce Paper-Writing Anxiety

Some students love to write papers; others dread the writing process. But almost all students will face writing situations in which they struggle to pick a topic, have difficulty developing an argument, or just can't seem to get started. For many college students, the writing process feels overwhelming, especially at the beginning when they're staring at a blank page. So if you're feeling some anxiety at the thought of writing a paper, you're not alone. The following strategies can help reduce that anxiety.

Before You Start Writing

Before you begin the paper, you can do a number of things to help you focus on the task ahead and get yourself going. Knowing how to get the writing process started will also keep you calm.

Pick a topic that interests you. Writing about something you find interesting makes the writing process much easier and more engaging. If you struggle to find a topic you like, talk to an instructor, a writing tutor, or a peer. Discussing possible topics may help you make meaningful connections that inspire you.

Establish your argument. Start by figuring out your main argument. Then, write a one- or two-sentence thesis that lays out what you plan to argue in the paper. Writing a thesis is important because it's the blueprint of your paper. A thesis tells the reader what your argument is and how you plan to prove it. To help you develop a thesis, think about why the topic interested you in the first place. What made it compelling, and why? Can you clearly articulate a meaningful argument about this topic? Can you support your argument with evidence?

Write a thorough outline. Writing an outline allows you to add detail to your thesis and determine the structure of the paper without worrying about making the prose beautiful. Writing an outline jump-starts the thinking process so that you can begin to figure out the argument and supporting evidence for your paper. An outline gives clear direction to your writing, making the writing process feel more manageable and reducing your anxiety about writing. A completed outline is also reassuring because you can see that you do, in fact, have something to say about a particular topic.

Take time to freewrite. If you're stuck and can't get going, take some time to freewrite about the topic. Remember: the first draft of your paper doesn't have to be perfect. You will stifle your own writing if you put too much pressure on yourself to get the first draft exactly right. To get your juices flowing, just start typing words on the screen that are in some way related to your topic and thesis.

> **QUICK TIP**
>
> ### Make Free-Writing a Conversation
> When you freewrite, pretend that you're talking to someone about the topic you picked. What's on your mind? What do you want to say? What are you hoping to prove or disprove? Why is the topic important to you? This technique will help you articulate your argument more clearly.

While You're Writing

You can take some steps *during* the paper-writing process to reduce any anxiety you may have. The following strategies will make the writing process feel more manageable; will help you write in your own voice; and will show you how to write more effectively and efficiently.

Break it down. Don't focus on writing the entire paper in one sitting, which can feel overwhelming and make it difficult to get started. Instead, break up the paper into smaller tasks, and build in refreshing breaks to keep you energized. For example, complete the first paragraph, and then take a ten-minute break. Tackle the next two paragraphs, and take another short break. The more you can break down the writing process into smaller chunks, the easier it will be to fill those blank pages.

Write in your own voice. Your instructor wants to see *your* voice, thoughts, and arguments in a paper, not your classmates' or your teaching assistant's ideas. If you use words that you barely understand or write phrases that sound false, the paper will not ring true for anyone, including you.

Read your writing aloud. To check whether your writing makes sense, is articulated clearly, and sounds like you, read it out loud. Do this regularly throughout the writing process. If a phrase or a sentence doesn't sound right, rework it so that you like what you hear. If you're stuck writing a paragraph, read what you have written out loud, and then keep talking to see if you can clearly state what you're trying to say. Also read aloud for friends or others to test your writing. It may be a little scary to read your writing in front of other people, but ask for their honest feedback—it will improve your writing.

Cite your sources as you write. If you're writing a paper that uses any sources, cite your sources whenever you use quotations in your paper or incorporate any ideas that are not your own. It's important to cite your sources as you write—otherwise, you might forget which words and ideas are your own and which come from your sources. Take the time to put the author's name and page number in parentheses after a quotation or at the end of a sentence if you include someone else's words or thoughts. See the following section for more details about citing your sources.

QUICK TIP

Keep Your Sources Sorted

Research papers can be especially challenging if you're incorporating many sources. One strategy is to go through all your sources and type out relevant quotations or ideas you'd like to incorporate in your paper, along with citations for each source. That way, you won't have to constantly go back to the sources to find what you're looking for.

Cite Your Sources

Whenever you use research in a college paper, you must cite the source of this research. You must also give credit to authors or anyone else if you include their ideas in your paper. Always cite the source of any words or ideas that are not your own, including research you find on Internet sites.

> **✓ CHECKLIST FOR REDUCING WRITING ANXIETY**
>
> ☐ Pick a paper topic that interests you.
> ☐ Figure out your main argument and write a thesis.
> ☐ Write a thorough outline of the paper.
> ☐ Freewrite to get started.
> ☐ Break the paper into smaller chunks.
> ☐ Take breaks frequently.
> ☐ Write in your own voice.
> ☐ Read your writing out loud.
> ☐ Cite your sources as you write.

Avoid Plagiarism

If you fail to give credit to your sources, you are plagiarizing. Plagiarizing is using other people's words or ideas without revealing where they came from. You must cite your sources not only when you quote someone else's words but also when you use someone else's arguments, evidence, or ideas. If you're caught plagiarizing, even if you claim that you weren't aware of any wrongdoing or thought you were citing properly, you can get into serious trouble—from failing the course to being expelled. Plagiarism is a serious offense, so you must take it seriously.

Most colleges have a code of conduct that explicitly defines plagiarism, outlines expectations for academic honesty, and lists the consequences for breaking those rules. Familiarize yourself with this code of conduct so that you know exactly what your college expects of students.

Use an Accepted Citation Style

Not all classes will follow the same citation guidelines, but all instructors will expect you to cite your sources. Usually, a course syllabus details the preferred citation

srizelda

' YOU'VE COPIED ALL THIS OFF
THE INTERNET... '

It's fine to quote sources in your paper, as long as you cite those sources properly. But if your paper is filled with other writers' ideas and you're having trouble writing in your own words, get help from your instructor or the writing center. Don't hand in a paper whose words and ideas come mostly (or solely!) from another source. College instructors expect you to write papers that show your own critical thinking.

style for the class; if not, be sure to ask your instructor. Humanities courses often use MLA (Modern Language Association) style or *The Chicago Manual of Style*, while science and social science courses usually use APA (American Psychological Association) style or a style guide geared for engineering or science writing. Make sure you know what citation style each instructor expects you to use, and have the appropriate style guide with you when you are working on assignments so that you can refer to it regularly.

QUICK TIP

Better Safe Than Sorry

If you have any questions about whether and when you need to cite sources, ask your instructor or a reference librarian, or meet with an advisor at the Academic Advising Office or writing center.

Technology and Information Literacy

Technology has transformed the way we perform research. The Internet has increased the amount of information flowing between people. All sorts of resources are now available online, including journal articles, newspapers, documentaries, dictionaries, maps, photographs, and videos. Resources that formerly existed only in hard copy, including entire books, are now online. Anyone can post information in the form of blogs, Wikipedia entries, or personal Web sites, even if they aren't experts. Libraries are becoming more and more digitized, and using search engines like Google, you can find information on almost any topic.

Navigating the World of Research Technology

The Internet provides powerful online research tools. In college, you'll be asked to use research in writing assignments, projects, and class discussions, so you need to know how to conduct research on the Internet appropriately. Not all information you find on the Internet is trustworthy. You need to know how to determine which sources are credible and which are not.

Evaluate online sources.   Google is a powerful tool, but use it wisely. Using search engines to find information can be a good starting point, but you must evaluate the results carefully. Many online sources of data haven't been vetted by experts in a field, so it's sometimes difficult to know whether the information you find is accurate or credible. If you want to use research from the Internet and are uncertain about its quality, check with a reference librarian or your instructor before you use it. Your instructor might also specify which Internet sources are okay to use and which are not.

For example, your instructor might not allow you to use research found on Wikipedia, a widely used online encyclopedia. Wikipedia articles are written collaboratively by volunteers and can be edited by anyone, so the information presented may or may not be accurate, depending on how knowledgeable the authors are about the topic.

Assess Web site credibility. One way to quickly assess the credibility of a Web site is to check the domain extension, or the last letters of the site, such as .com, .org, .gov, or .edu. A Web site address ending in .com usually indicates a commercial or business site. Most of these sites are trying to sell something and want to shed a positive light on the product being promoted, so alternative views usually are not represented. If the Web site address ends in .org, the site is usually sponsored by an organization or a not-for-profit association that is offering credible information. But information presented on .org sites might be biased, depending on the Web site sponsor. Web sites with addresses ending in .gov or .edu are considered the most credible because the information provided on the sites comes from the federal government or educational institutions.

Cite online sources carefully. In college papers, you must cite all your sources, including sources you find on the Internet. Consult a style guide to find out how to cite online sources, both in the body of your paper and in a list of works cited at the end of the paper.

Use Electronic Resources at the Library

College library Web sites provide a number of electronic resources. You'll find research tools that connect you to millions of journal articles, newspapers, books, archived information, and more. Take the time to explore what electronic resources the library offers—especially because those sources are likely to be credible—and to learn how to navigate your library's online system.

Librarians are a trusted resource. Be sure to speak with a reference librarian, who can assist you as you navigate the library's electronic research databases. Library staff not only can save you time but can also point you in the right direction if you're not sure where to start your research.

Don't forget about printed books. We often use computers to do research, but don't forget to look at the printed books in your college library. Although your library may have many digitized books online, you might find good sources for your assignment in the pages of a printed book. So take the time to browse the library's shelves.

Visual Walkthrough

Your College Library Is a Vast Resource

For many of your class assignments, you will need to do a lot of research. To discover what resources your college library offers, check out its Web site. Not only will you be able to find a vast array of sources online and in print, but you can also communicate with experienced librarians who can assist you in your research.

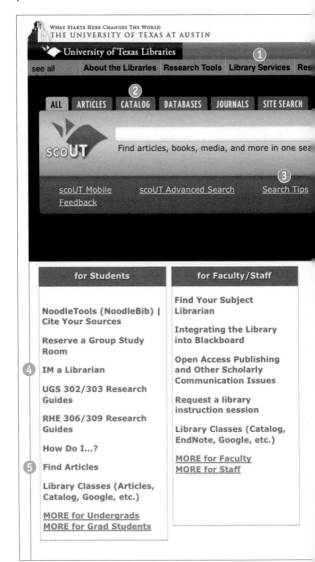

1. Discover all the services your library has to offer, including information about borrowing books and other sources, interlibrary loan, copying and printing, study spaces, library tutorials, and much more.

2. Your library has vast online and print resources. By searching the entire catalog, you can tap into a wide variety of sources, including online journals and magazines, e-books, printed books, CDs, and DVDs.

3. Use search tips to narrow down your topic, making it easier to focus on the most relevant and useful sources.

4. Text, e-mail, call, or visit a librarian whenever you have a question or for general advice on searching, finding appropriate sources, and how to use the library most effectively.

5. At the click of a button, you can search for articles from journals, magazines, and newspapers on almost any topic.

Chapter 10
Academic Planning, Majors, and Careers

A s a first-year student, you need to start thinking about academic planning, which will be an ongoing process throughout your time at college. You might not yet know what you want to study, or you might have already decided what field of study you want to focus on. Either way, if you want to succeed in college, you need to develop a plan for how you will fulfill any general academic requirements, complete your major and minor course requirements, determine a balanced course load, and choose classes you enjoy.

Selecting Courses

You should put a great deal of thought into selecting your courses. Fortunately, you do not have to make these decisions alone. As you learned in Chapter 1, you will be assigned an academic advisor who will work with you on short-term and long-term academic planning. Your advisor is an important sounding board and an integral part of your decision-making process. You can also take advantage of many other academic resources available on campus, such as the Academic Advising Office, the First-Year Programs Office, and specific academic departments.

You will work closely with your advisor on course selection, but you may need to turn to other professionals on campus if you have questions your advisor can't answer, if you'd like an additional perspective on courses, or if you need help immediately and your advisor isn't available. It's up to you to find answers to your questions. Fortunately, colleges often provide a number of academic resources that can assist you.

Combine Your Interests with Requirements

Talk with your advisor about your interests and general academic requirements. Which majors do you want to explore during your first year? If you are already excited about a specific subject, go ahead and check out the class description in the course catalog before meeting with your advisor. This way, you can discover in advance which classes, within these fields, appeal to you. And do the same if you already know what you'd like to major in. Also check whether your college has required courses that all students have to take; most colleges do. What academic requirements do you need to keep in mind as you start mapping out your classes and academic plan? If you're at a two-year college and plan to transfer, figure out what courses you need to take in order to make this transition, and be sure they are part of your academic plan.

Each college is different in terms of course selection, required courses, and how many courses students can take each term. Take time to *fully* understand what is required for graduation or what is recommended if you plan to transfer to another school later on. Your advisor understands the intricacies of the academic system and can help you decide which courses might be appropriate for you, based on your interests and college require- ments. And if you are returning to school after a break in your education, your advisor will help you determine what courses you need to take to complete your degree, taking into consideration any prior college credits you have.

Map Out Your Academic Plan

A balanced course load is a key to success in college. If possible, create a mixture of courses that provides variety in terms of the subjects represented and the type of work that will be performed in each class (such as reading, writing, problem sets, labs, or projects). In addition, try to mix the difficulty level of your courses, choosing some classes that are more challenging than others. If possible, don't pick courses that are all difficult or all easy. Be sure to talk to your advisor about how to put together a balanced course load.

With your academic interests and requirements in mind, map out a first-year academic plan with the help of your advisor. Start with any required courses that you must take during your first year. Then, add some classes from majors that you'd like to explore or appropriate classes from the major you know you'll be pursuing. Keep your course load balanced in terms of work assigned, subject matter, and difficulty level. And if you end up with an unbalanced course load, which is sometimes unavoidable, talk with your advisor or someone at the Academic Advising Office if you find yourself struggling.

Whether or not you know your major yet, try to determine when you will take your additional requirements during the remainder of college. You can certainly change your mind at a later date, but making these long-term plans now can make your future academic planning easier. You don't want to have to take several required courses in your final year of college!

If you're fairly certain of your major/minor, you can determine when you might take your major/minor classes as you're mapping out your long-term academic plan. But if you're exploring a few majors during your first year, you should narrow down your subject interests (usually after one or two terms) before attempting to do this.

Remember, no one can read your mind. Your advisor can help you grapple with selecting courses *only* if you tell him or her what your interests are and whether you're struggling to make a decision. You also need to tell your advisor about your life situation. If you are juggling course work while also raising a family, or if you are going to school at night while holding down a full-time job, you might need to spread your course work over a longer period of time. Picking courses each term can be a bit of a puzzle; but if you discuss with your advisor which classes you're interested in, which course requirements you need to fulfill each term, and how your life situation might affect your course load, the two of you can find a solution to that puzzle.

Visual Walkthrough

Balance Your Course Load

Picking courses requires a lot of thought as you try to balance your interests and any required courses and as you explore your major or minor. You're also aiming for a balance in the type of courses you take each term.

A Poorly Balanced Course Load

Term 1 ①	Term 2 ②
Organic Chemistry (pre-med requirement)	World History (general requirement)
Physics 1 (pre-med requirement)	Modern American Literature (possible minor)
General Biology (pre-med requirement)	College Writing (general requirement)
Introduction to Astronomy (general requirement)	Sociology 100 (possible major)
Calculus A (pre-med requirement)	Conversational Spanish (fulfills foreign-language requirement)

A More Balanced Course Load

Term 1	Term 2
Organic Chemistry (pre-med requirement)	World History (general requirement)
④ Studies in American Culture (possible minor)	Physics 1 (pre-med requirement) ③
③ College Writing (general requirement)	General Biology (pre-med requirement)
Introduction to Astronomy (general requirement)	Sociology 100 (possible major)
⑤ Calculus A (pre-med requirement)	Conversational Spanish (fulfills foreign language requirement)

1. Try not to take only science and math courses in one term, especially as a first-year student. You might be overwhelmed by doing similar work all the time — problem sets, labs, memorization. You also won't have variety in what you're studying, which is a problem if you would like to explore different majors.

2. Try not to take only reading- and writing-based courses at once. Taking these courses in the same term would be particularly challenging, given the amount of required reading and the number of papers that would be assigned in these courses.

3. You can create a more balanced course load by figuring out which classes are offered several times during the school year. Physics I, General Biology, and College Writing are offered both terms, so you have flexibility as to when you can take them, allowing you to balance your course load.

4. Modern American Literature is offered only in the second term. A similar English course, Studies in American Culture, is offered only in the first term. Given that you are interested in both courses, you might want to choose one over the other in a particular term in order to create a more balanced course load.

5. If you are a pre-med student and need to fulfill course requirements that will allow you to apply to medical school, talk to your advisor about fitting these requirements into your academic plan. In addition, check whether some of the pre-med courses might also count for other college requirements.

Keep Your Advisor in the Loop

Schedule regular meetings with your advisor through-out the year to discuss how things are going. How do you like your classes? Which classes do you find most interesting or most surprising? Which classes don't you enjoy? Does the course load feel manageable? If not, where are you struggling, and how can you get the help you need to succeed? Be honest with your advisor so that you get the advice you need and can make the most of each term.

Be Smart about Class Exploration

Choosing classes isn't always easy, especially if you are interested in several majors. The choices can seem endless. And colleges often give you many options when it comes to required classes. You might be tempted to pick classes based on what sounds most interesting or what other students have recommended. But keep a few factors in mind as you map out your academic plan.

Be realistic about your preparedness. Every high school is unique. Your preparation for college might differ from that of other students because you're all from different school systems, communities, and families. If you graduated from a high school that offered few honors or AP classes, or if you didn't take college prep course work, you might face greater academic challenges in college than other students. And if you're returning to college after a break in your education, you may feel further behind or more rusty than those who are going straight through. Acknowledging your specific chal-lenges can help you pick courses with an eye to increasing your success.

Don't jump into advanced course work unless you have the appropriate background. If you have never taken a psychology course before, take an introductory course before you attempt an advanced course. Work with your advisor to determine what a balanced course load looks like *for you*. Do not compare yourself to peers.

Everyone has different academic interests and strengths, so no two course loads will look the same. The academic tools you bring to college matter as a point of information, but they aren't a reflection of your potential.

Share Your History

Talk with your instructor during the first week of class if you haven't had any exposure to the subject matter, didn't have a good experience in a relevant AP class, or are returning to the classroom after a break in your education. Make sure the instructor is aware of your background in the subject in case you find the class particularly challenging. Ask about strategies to help you succeed in the class, such as visiting the instructor during office hours or getting a tutor. You may realize that you need to work much harder than other students in your class.

Consider how challenged you'll be. You'll certainly be challenged in college, but it's important to ask yourself how many challenging classes you can handle. This question is especially relevant as you balance your course load. A few challenging courses in a term can be intellectually stimulating, but too many can be intellectually overwhelming. If you're not sure about the difficulty level of a class, talk to your advisor and to students who have taken the course. The instructor for the class can also let you know what's expected and how much time you need to spend on class assignments to be successful.

When a course is too difficult. Even with the right academic preparation, you may find that a course you've chosen is very difficult and that no matter how much effort you put in, you still struggle. If so, talk to your instructor and go to the Academic Advising Office to find out what you can do to help yourself. Consider working with a tutor so that you can go over the material one-on-one. If you continue to struggle and are worried that you might fail, you may be able to withdraw from the course, depending on how far into the term you are. But be sure to find out what a withdrawal could mean for your academic standing. Check the college's rules regarding withdrawing from a class, and speak immediately with your advisor, especially if the class is a requirement for graduation or a requirement for your major.

QUICK TIP

Learn from Your Struggles

If you struggle in a class or get a bad grade even though you put in a lot of effort, keep that in mind when you're choosing courses for the next term. Picking different types of courses doesn't mean you're a failure; it usually means that certain material is particularly challenging and that other subjects might be more suited to your strengths and interests.

---

⑤ MISTAKES SMART FIRST-YEAR STUDENTS SOMETIMES MAKE

1. **Taking a class because a friend thought it was easy.**

   Everyone has different strengths and weaknesses. Listen to your friend's opinion, but do your own research on the class as well.

2. **Exploring classes or a degree program that only your mom, dad, or partner is interested in.**

   Resisting outside influences and pressure can be difficult, but you're the one who will be in class day after day.

3. **Taking an online course because you thought it would be easier.**

   Online courses can be just as challenging as regular courses. Before enrolling, be sure that you're actually interested in the class or are fulfilling a requirement.

4. **Deciding to get the "tough classes" out of the way.**

   Taking too many challenging classes at once can cause burnout and might lower your performance and your GPA.

5. **Taking more than the recommended number of courses to "get ahead."**

   Taking a heavy course load might be doable, but first figure out how to manage a normal course load. A heavy course load can leave you feeling overwhelmed, especially if you have a lot going on in your personal life.

Understand Online Course Registration

In college, you'll use an online course registration system to sign up for courses each term and to change the status of your courses if necessary. For example, you might decide to add or drop a course, withdraw from a course, or change the grading status of a class. All of these changes can be made through your college's course registration Web site. Always consult with your advisor before registering for any courses online or making course status changes. Your advisor can also help you navigate the course registration system if you have questions.

If you're interested in taking a limited-enrollment class (in which the instructor has limited the number of students who can enroll), check how the online course registration system will inform you that you've been accepted into the class, that you've been placed on a waiting list for the class (and that you've been moved from the waiting list to the list of enrolled students), or that you haven't gotten into the class. You want to be sure

---

✓ **CHECKLIST FOR SELECTING COURSES**

☐ Combine your interests and academic requirements.

☐ Consider what required courses you'll need if you plan to transfer.

☐ Map out both a short-term and a long-term academic plan.

☐ Work closely with your academic advisor.

☐ Find a course load that balances subject matter, the amount of work assigned, and difficulty.

☐ Factor in your personal commitments (such as taking care of or supporting a family) when determining a balanced course load.

☐ Be realistic about your level of preparedness.

☐ Consider how challenged you'll be.

☐ Understand how to use the online course registration system.

that you're taking the right number of courses or credits each term, so use the online course registration system to check that you're actually enrolled in the classes.

Choose a Major That Is Right for You

Choosing your major is a key decision in college. Your major defines what your academic life will look like, especially during the last few years of college, so you want to choose a major that is right for you.

Balance Your Goals and Interests

Some students enter college with a definite career path in mind. Others don't know what career they will pursue after graduation. Either way, you want to major in something you enjoy, at least somewhat. If you have always wanted to go into business but dislike most, if not all, of your economics and business-related classes, you probably should consider another major. You might still pursue a career in business, but you'll be much happier during your college years if you study something you like, enhancing your health and well-being. In addition, the more you enjoy the classes in your major, the more likely you are to work harder, improving your overall academic performance.

Consider a Minor

If you want to study a few different academic fields in depth, consider minoring in one of them. Minoring in a subject can be a great way to fulfill your interests and may be easier than you think. In fact, toward the end of college, students are sometimes surprised to discover that they can declare a minor in a field because they've taken enough classes in the academic discipline to fulfill the requirements.

Colleges often allow students to double-major or even triple-major. Majoring in two or three fields is another way to combine many academic interests.

" Of course, I'm argumentative . . I'm PRE-LAW, for goodness sake ! "

▲

When picking your major field of study, consider whether that major will be a good fit with your characteristics, strengths, interests, and skills.

However, talk extensively with your advisor about this decision—you want to be sure you are able to take on this type of academic challenge, especially if you are balancing family, work, and school commitments. And check that you have enough time to complete the required courses in the majors you are pursuing.

It's Okay to Be Undecided

If you are undecided about your major or minor and are nervous about finding an academic path suited to your interests, you are not alone. Many students attend college not knowing what they want to study. Figuring out your academic interests can take time, especially given the many options available. Don't feel pressured about making your major or minor decision within the first few months on campus. Usually, you do have time to explore your interests, so be sure to keep an open mind throughout this exploratory process.

If you take a variety of courses during your first term and don't think any are right for you as a major, don't worry. Trial and error is inevitable. You can try out different classes in the next term or the one after that. In fact, discovering that you *don't* like a particular class or a certain subject is as valuable as finding one you do like. The key to college success is being able to pinpoint what field excites you. When you study what interests you, you will work harder, enjoy the process more, and perform better.

QUICK TIP

Keep an Open Mind

You might be quite sure of your academic interests upon entering college, but you also might surprise yourself. It's fine if you think you know what you want to study as soon as you step foot on campus, but you might want to challenge yourself to explore other options. Fortunately, with so many academic disciplines to choose from, you will be able to find your individual path to success. So, while a particular major or minor might prove too challenging, be open-minded as you discover what other disciplines are a better fit.

It's Okay to Change Your Mind

Many college students declare a major or pursue a specific degree path and then decide later that it's not right for them. If you have a change of heart regarding your major (and if it's early enough for you to switch majors), be sure to meet with your advisor or someone at the Academic Advising Office to determine what steps you need to take to switch majors. Find out whether the classes you've taken will count toward your new major or whether you have to take additional classes in a term to be able to graduate on time.

If you find out that you can't change majors easily, ask your advisor whether you can minor in the field that interests you, or take a heavier load for a few terms, or take summer courses, or graduate later than you anticipated. These are all difficult roads, so talk with your advisor to determine if switching your major is worth it. And if it's too late to switch majors, you probably should stick with your original academic plan in order to graduate on time; however, it might be possible to take more electives in your preferred subject area.

Recognize Career Influences

Your major will probably influence your career decisions. Whether or not you have a career focus when you enter college, you might find that the intellectual exploration you encounter within your major broadens your interests and opens up new possibilities for careers. You will experience a lot of personal and intellectual growth during college: your academic experiences might reinforce your previous career goals, alter your career trajectory, or completely change your career interests. Take time to be introspective throughout college so that you can discover what career options truly interest you.

 CASE STUDY

Kim shares her experience choosing classes, balancing her course load, and picking her majors.

I determined which classes I took each term based on a number of factors. I always checked to see whether classes fell within the general requirements of the university or whether they fell under the requirements for either of my majors, and how often they were offered. The university offered some courses only every other year or every third year.

I met with my advisor quite often in the beginning of my college years. Figuring out a balanced course load took some time to get right. I often found myself with too many paper-based courses in one term rather than a couple of paper-based courses and a couple of exam-based courses. I took a few classes just to take them, but I don't think that was a mistake. A few classes sounded a lot better on paper than they actually were, though. After that experience, I read course descriptions more carefully and asked students who had taken the class previously.

Drop-in hours at the Academic Advising Office were probably the most helpful type of academic planning service. I determined my majors by what kind of classes I took. I realized how much I loved writing, and therefore English became my first major. Sociology became my second major. I took a few sociology classes and realized that I could major in it if I took classes in the summer.

QUESTIONS FOR REFLECTION: Do you think you've found a good balance of courses? Why or why not? When you choose your courses for future terms, what might you do differently?

Career Planning

For most students, college is a time to prepare for a future in the workforce. You can choose from many job and career options, and colleges have resources to help you navigate this wider world. Career offices offer career counseling, help with writing résumés and cover letters, assistance with finding internships and summer positions, and help conducting a job search and applying for available positions. (See Chapter 15 for more information about career planning.) Many colleges also offer similar types of support for alumni.

Visit the Career Services Office during your first year to explore the resources that it offers. You might not feel the need to meet with a counselor at this point, but if you familiarize yourself with the Career Services Office during your first year, you'll be more likely to seek assistance later on.

Whether you are undecided or fairly certain about your career path, talking to a career counselor will help you understand how your interests, personality, and strengths might fit certain careers. Counselors are important sounding boards who know what jobs and internships are available and who can help you determine whether they might interest you. Internship and job experiences are also available and provide a window into career fields and work environments, allowing you to narrow down what you do and don't like.

Chapter 11
Staying Healthy and Reducing Stress

Two ways to improve your college experience are staying healthy and finding ways to reduce stress. Keeping both your mind and your body in good shape will make it easier to manage your college schedule, concentrate in class, study effectively, and perform well on exams. The suggestions in this chapter will help you figure out how to balance college life while also taking good care of yourself.

Eat, Sleep, and Exercise

In college, it's important to try to keep your body fueled, to stick to a regular sleep schedule, and to stay physically active. This may seem like simple advice, but staying healthy in college often falls by the wayside when you are coping with a busy schedule, large volumes of work, and exams.

Keep Your Body Fueled

Be sure to make mealtimes a regular part of your routine. Whether you're eating in food courts and dining halls on campus, cooking for yourself, or going out for a meal, be sure to eat food that satisfies you, keeps you energized during class, and fuels your brain while studying and completing assignments. When your brain is working at the high levels required in college, you are expending a lot of energy, and you need enough nourishing fuel to keep you going.

Pick healthy options. Try to eat at least two or three healthy meals a day. What constitutes a "healthy meal"? It's a balanced meal that consists of protein of some sort, carbohydrates (whole-grain foods are best), and lots of fruits and vegetables.

Start the day off right. Every morning, be sure to eat a nutritious breakfast. If you don't have time to go to the dining hall, keep fruit, nuts, bagels, or cereal readily available. If you tend to sleep through classes or always

Visual Walkthrough

Making Balanced Food Choices

In college, you can grab a meal in many places —
whether it's the late-night pizza place, the café in the
library, or your own refrigerator. Throughout the
hustle and bustle of each day, try to choose a variety
of healthy foods, with a balance of fruits, vegetables,
grains, and protein.

① When you're on the go, easy fruit options include
apples, bananas, and grapes. And fruit smoothies
can be particularly satisfying.

② Vegetables might not be your favorite food, but raw
carrots are a great snack. Other healthy options
include hummus, raw broccoli, celery, asparagus,
and zucchini. If you make your own smoothies or
shakes, add a handful of spinach or kale.

③ You need good carbohydrates to get you through
the day, so grab a granola bar, use whole-grain
bread for sandwiches, and eat a healthy cereal in
the morning.

4. You can find protein not only in chicken, pork, fish, and beef but also in eggs, beans, and nuts.

5. Dairy products are great sources of calcium and protein, so pick up string cheese, add milk to your cereal, and eat a cup of yogurt a day. If you are dairy-free, almond milk, soy milk, and rice milk are all good alternatives.

feel tired, that sluggishness might be a sign that you're not eating anything in the morning. Eating a good breakfast will perk you up.

Stay well fueled all day. Eat snacks between meals. In college, you're always on the go, so be sure to eat a snack that keeps your energy levels up. Grab whatever satisfies you—a banana, a granola bar, a cup of yogurt—and have it ready when you need a pick-me-up.

Monitor caffeine intake. Enjoy caffeinated beverages, but find the right balance. You might feel that you need coffee or soda to get through the day, but if you overdo it, you might find it difficult to concentrate. Be aware of how much caffeine you're consuming. If you consume too much caffeine, you can feel jittery rather than energized.

> **QUICK TIP**
>
> ### Talk to Someone
>
> If you're eating a lot more than you think you should and you can't control yourself, talk to someone. Similarly, if you're eating a lot less than you think you should, talk to someone. Get help from your mentor, an advisor, or the counseling office. An eating disorder could be a sign that you're struggling with other aspects of college life, so be sure to ask for help.

Eating well is pretty simple if you make it a priority. Healthy foods can improve both your energy level and your ability to concentrate, so be sure to fit in a healthy diet during your college years.

Find a Sleep Solution

In college, some students find that they're sleeping more than ever because they don't have morning classes. Other students may sleep less than normal because they are juggling so many things. Yet others experience shifts in their sleep schedules—sometimes they stay up all night and then sleep during the day. Whatever your sleep preferences, take some time when you begin college to figure out a sleep pattern that works best for you.

Sleep—or lack of sleep—can have a significant impact on your energy level and your ability to concentrate. Are you most productive when you stay up late to study and complete assignments? If so, can you still stay attentive in class? Or do you find that you can't even stay awake during the lecture?

Try to find a sleep schedule that makes you feel productive and energized. You may not be able to get eight hours of sleep a night, but try to sleep at least six or seven hours. Maybe an afternoon nap will fill the sleep deficit. Occasionally, you may need to pull an all-nighter—for example, before a test or when a paper is due. But as soon as you can, try to get back to a regular sleep pattern.

QUICK TIP

Get Enough Sleep

Not getting enough sleep could be an indication that you're engaged in too many activities, that your course load is too heavy, or that you're struggling to fit in job hours. Rather than reducing your hours of sleep, try cutting back on something else. And talk to a trusted college advisor or mentor if you're really struggling to get enough sleep.

Exercise Can Make All the Difference

One thing that can enhance your well-being in college is exercise. Physical activity of all kinds relieves tension and stress, provides needed oxygen to your body, and gives your active brain a much-needed break. You don't have to go to the gym seven days a week to get the benefits of exercise. Once you find a physical activity that you enjoy, engage in it four or five times a week. You'll feel better—and you'll perform better in college.

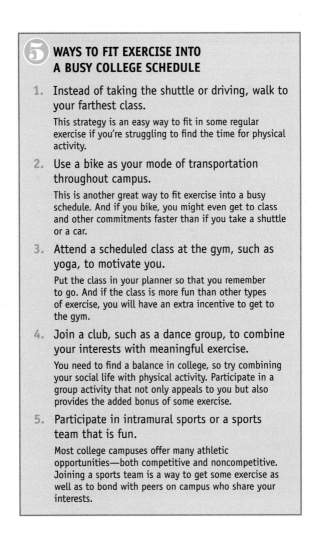

⑤ WAYS TO FIT EXERCISE INTO A BUSY COLLEGE SCHEDULE

1. **Instead of taking the shuttle or driving, walk to your farthest class.**

   This strategy is an easy way to fit in some regular exercise if you're struggling to find the time for physical activity.

2. **Use a bike as your mode of transportation throughout campus.**

   This is another great way to fit exercise into a busy schedule. And if you bike, you might even get to class and other commitments faster than if you take a shuttle or a car.

3. **Attend a scheduled class at the gym, such as yoga, to motivate you.**

   Put the class in your planner so that you remember to go. And if the class is more fun than other types of exercise, you will have an extra incentive to get to the gym.

4. **Join a club, such as a dance group, to combine your interests with meaningful exercise.**

   You need to find a balance in college, so try combining your social life with physical activity. Participate in a group activity that not only appeals to you but also provides the added bonus of some exercise.

5. **Participate in intramural sports or a sports team that is fun.**

   Most college campuses offer many athletic opportunities—both competitive and noncompetitive. Joining a sports team is a way to get some exercise as well as to bond with peers on campus who share your interests.

Manage Your Stress

Stress is a fact of life in college, especially during your first year when everything is new. You may experience stress for many different reasons. Maybe you're away from home for the first time or are trying to balance college classes with a demanding job and family life. Perhaps you don't understand material in certain classes and are struggling to choose your major. Extracurricular activities or a sports commitment might be more demanding than you expected. Given that you will probably experience some stress in college, you need to be able to manage it effectively.

Build a Community

It is important to build a community of people on campus you trust. Find instructors, advisors, or mentors you can talk to about the ups and downs of your college experience so that they can assist you. Seek out students whom you feel you can connect to. It takes time to build true friendships, but if you make the effort to join a club that fits your interests, you can meet other students with similar interests. Participate in events that bring together people from your culture, religion, or ethnicity. Take the initiative in building a support system that is there when you need it.

Stay Connected

It may take a while to find support on campus; until you do, manage your stress by staying in touch with family, friends, and mentors from your pre-college life. If you're struggling with classes and haven't yet found an advisor, call the teacher who always looked out for you in high school. When you need to talk to someone who really understands you, call your best friend or a sibling. We all derive strength and hope from others, so reach out to someone when you need to. Staying connected is essential for your mental health.

"They've all tested positive for stress."

▲

Most college students experience varying amounts of stress throughout college. Try a few different ways to reduce stress to see what works for you. And remember that you're not alone— you can get help from campus resources such as the counseling center whenever you need help managing your stress.

Be Good to Yourself

To alleviate anxiety and tension and maintain a sense of calm, incorporate the following suggestions into your lifestyle.

Stay healthy. The more you maintain a healthy lifestyle, the more you can reduce your stress levels. Eat nutritious foods that you enjoy; take a nap, if it will help you make it through the day; go to the gym; or get some exercise outdoors. Physical activity can melt away stress, at least for a short time. If stress is making you anxious and short of breath, physical activity will help you breathe more easily. Even tensing and relaxing muscles while at your computer can help.

Stay organized. Disorganization can cause unnecessary stress. If you're always late to meetings because you forget to write them down in your planner or if you keep losing class syllabi because you stick them in a messy pile of papers on your desk, you're adding stress to your life. If you start practicing the time management strategies discussed in Chapter 2, you'll be able to stay organized and to keep track of your schedule, course requirements, and commitments.

Take breaks. In college, you're always on the go and might forget to take some time to relax. No matter whether you're engaged in a marathon study session, writing a ten-page paper, or in the midst of rehearsing for an upcoming performance, you need to take an occasional break and recharge your batteries. Go outside in the fresh air. Enjoy a snack. Listen to your favorite music. Call a friend. Read a book for enjoyment. Watch your favorite TV show.

Do something brainless. When you work your brain too much, you can become stressed and tired. Do something that doesn't require you to think for a while. Do some spring cleaning, listen to your favorite music, go to a movie, or check Facebook.

Rest and relax. On weekends, give yourself permission to take a long break. Whether you escape for a few hours or for the whole afternoon, make time for true rest and relaxation. Take a hike or go on a short road trip. Meet friends for coffee and a movie. It doesn't matter what the activity is; just be sure that it leaves you feeling rested and relaxed.

Engage in activities you enjoy. Don't join clubs that just add more stress to your life. Instead, join activities that you love. In college, you have a wide variety of activities to choose from. Be sure to choose what *you* want to do, not what your friends are doing or what you think will build your résumé. Time is precious in college, and the time you spend on extracurricular activities should leave you feeling invigorated, not drained.

Reward yourself. Be sure to recognize your hard work in college, even if your grades don't always reflect your intellect and abilities. If you're putting your best effort into classes, papers, and studying, pat yourself on the back once in a while. College is a time of great personal growth. Reflect on how far you've come, the challenges you're facing, and how much you're doing and learning. Be good to yourself—give yourself some sort of reward, such as an ice cream sundae or a concert on campus.

Get help from campus resources. If you're feeling overwhelmed by stress, ask yourself why. Then decide whether your advisor or mentor might be able to help you find techniques for relieving the stress. Remember, you're never alone.

✓ CHECKLIST FOR STAYING HEALTHY

- [ ] Eat regularly, and choose healthy, balanced food options whenever possible.
- [ ] Make sleep a priority so that you get at least six or seven hours of sleep a night.
- [ ] Find physical activities that make you feel rejuvenated, and exercise regularly.
- [ ] Keep yourself organized to reduce unnecessary stress.
- [ ] Take breaks regularly so that your brain and body can rest and relax.
- [ ] Make time for activities that are fun and meaningful.
- [ ] Be kind to yourself, and find ways to reward yourself when you deserve recognition.
- [ ] Get help from campus resources if you're stressed or need to talk to someone about issues with eating, sleep, or exercise.

CASE STUDY

Alicia explains how she learned to manage her stress.

In college, my health suffered as a result of my stress levels. I experienced difficulty concentrating and suffered from anxiety that made it hard to sleep and eat. With support from my mentor and a few others, I decided to join a theater group and a dance team. I also started taking advantage of the health center on my campus and committed to weekly visits. I participated in a paid blogging-for-college opportunity that allowed me to share my college experience in a more positive light. I taught other students how to dance. I started to live for myself and to do things that brought joy into my life.

As a first-year college student, it is important to understand what you can do to manage the stress you will experience. I tried a variety of activities and recognized that if something doesn't work, try again; if it still doesn't work, try something new. People say that it's important to find your niche in college, and when I did, I found that I was better able to deal with stress that came my way.

QUESTIONS FOR REFLECTION: Have you found effective ways to manage the stress you've experienced in college? If so, what makes the biggest impact on reducing your stress? If you haven't yet found effective ways of dealing with stress, have you asked a mentor or an advisor for help?

Experiencing Difference

You will experience difference in many ways throughout college, including difference of opinions in class, divergent political views, and diversity of all types—race, religion, socioeconomic status, sexual orientation, and cultural background. However you define *diversity*, your college campus may have a lot of diversity or very little. Maybe you've never been exposed to various types of diversity, or maybe diversity is part of your daily life. Understanding how to work with and embrace differences in college will help you make the most of your experience and better prepare you for life after college.

Acknowledge Differences

The diversity you encounter will depend on your own background and your unique college experience. For example, your politics or your religion may differ from that of most students on campus. You may have to deal with differences if you're living with a roommate for the first time. If you don't live on campus, your experiences with difference might occur mainly in the classroom and through student activities.

Diversity involves more than race. In college, you will find diversity in socioeconomic status, cultural background, religion, age, and sexual orientation. For example, you may be one of just a few first-generation college students on campus, or you may be returning to school after some time in the workforce and are much older than most other students. If you identify with a specific culture or are part of the LGBT (lesbian, gay, bisexual, transgender) community, you may want to find ways to connect with others on campus and to find support.

You might feel that you fit in well and are comfortable on campus, or you might not. It often takes time to get acclimated, especially if you are in the minority in some way. It can take some effort to find your niche in college. Regardless of your comfort level during your first year, it's important to acknowledge the differences in your campus community and to consider what you can do to help yourself and others feel more comfortable when differences become apparent.

Keep an Open Mind

However you encounter diversity and difference at college, your past matters. If you come from a racially homogeneous school or community, much of the diversity you've encountered may be in the form of differences in personal preferences, interests in student activities and sports, or political opinions. If you're from a religiously or culturally homogeneous community, your first year in college may be the first time you're meeting individuals with divergent beliefs and cultural practices.

Keep in mind how your past may influence your reaction to the differences you encounter at college. You might feel apprehensive or nervous when meeting others from backgrounds different from your own, or you might be excited to learn about the diversity that exists. Keep an open mind as you get to know others from divergent backgrounds. Keeping an open mind doesn't mean that you will always agree with others, but it does mean that you'll listen carefully and recognize that other students' backgrounds have influenced who they are, just as your background has shaped you. The more you learn about others on a personal level, the more you'll see them for who they are, rather than making assumptions based on the "group" they are associated with.

Challenge Stereotypes

College presents an opportunity to become more comfortable with diversity of all types and also to challenge stereotypes. Sadly, stereotypes are prevalent in our society, and your preconceived notions about a particular culture, religion, or behavior may influence how you experience the diversity you encounter. Most of us do harbor stereotypes, even if they are subconscious judgments that we don't admit to. We often develop these stereotypes before we have been exposed to diversity, so college may push you in ways you never expected. Let it. Work toward challenging and overcoming the stereotypes you have brought with you to college. Remember that college is a time to open your mind not only to academic information but also to new ideas and a diversity of people.

Understand and Respect Difference

No matter what your background is, you can celebrate what makes each person unique, even as you make an effort to understand and respect differences. Find support around issues of diversity by engaging in meaningful activities and connecting with campus resources. It's also important to be open and willing to learn from our differences. The remainder of this chapter elaborates on both of these ideas.

Find Support on Campus

A number of resources on campus provide support around issues of diversity. If you are struggling to make connections at college, it can help to find others who have similar interests, beliefs, and experiences. Here are a few easy steps you can take to find a community of like-minded students.

Join Meaningful Clubs or Organizations

Many clubs and organizations on college campuses bring together like-minded students or students from a similar background. Examples include the Black Student Union, Arab Students Club, Latin American Network, Chinese Student Association, Native American Student Association, Campus Crusade for Christ, Asian American Campus Ministry, Jewish Student Union, Hindu Student Association, Pride Alliance, University Democrats, and College Republicans.

"Our goal is to stress di-versity while remaining a uni-versity."

Because students come from a wide variety of backgrounds, colleges often make efforts to acknowledge and celebrate difference and to offer support around diversity. These efforts help unify campuses by bridging differences, bringing diverse groups together, and openly addressing important diversity-related topics.

Understand the Greek Community

If you are interested in fraternities or sororities that have a specific focus or mission, take time to understand the cultures that exist within each Greek organization on campus and determine what is expected if you want to become a member. These organizations can provide opportunities to build strong connections with others and to give back to the community.

Look for Campus Resources

College campuses often have offices and committees dedicated to issues of diversity. You might come across resources such as the Center for Multicultural Advancement, Center for Women, Office of Diversity and Inclusion, Office of Multicultural Affairs, College Cultural Center, Veteran Services Office, Office of Religious and Spiritual Life, Disability Services Office, Diversity Advisory Committee, or Council on the Status of Diversity. Be sure to find out what services they offer.

Visual Walkthrough

Learn about Your College's Diversity Resources

Search your college's Web site to find out what services are offered around issues of diversity and difference. Find out what resources might benefit you, and make an effort to reach out by visiting the offices or clubs, meeting staff members, or interacting with peers who are involved.

Virginia Tech Principles of Community

Virginia Tech is a public land-grant university, committed to teaching and learning, research, and outreach to the Commonwealth of Virginia, the nation, and the world community. Learning from the experiences that shape Virginia Tech as an institution, we acknowledge those aspects of our legacy that reflected bias and exclusion.

Therefore, we adopt and practice our Principles of Community as fundamental to our on-going efforts to increase access and inclusion and to create a community that nurtures learning and growth for all of its members.

» Read the entire Principles of Community statement

1 ### Office for Diversity and Inclusion

The Office for Diversity and Inclusion envisions a university committed to building a community of excellence through the affirmation of difference.

Task Force on Race and the Institution

The task force, convened in October 2006, is examining issues of race and racism at Virginia Tech, with a goal of identifying key issues and proposing specific actions that will enhance our opportunities to make lasting progress.

Student Overview

See a breakdown of the student population by race and gender.

2 ### Academic Programs

Programs whose focus is the study of traditionally underserved populations.

Growing and Sustaining a Diverse and Inclusive Environment

» The 2010-2013 Virginia Tech Diversity Strategic Plan (PDF | 133KB)

University Organizations

» For faculty/staff
- Black Faculty and Staff Caucus
- Hispanic Faculty Staff Caucus
- Lesbian, Gay, Bisexual, and Transgender Caucus
- Veterans at Virginia Tech

3 » For students

Documents & Reports

The Provost's website archive includes extensive records of Virginia Tech's ongoing commitment to campus diversity and multiculturalism.

4 ### Campus Resources

Programs and services for the diverse campus community.

5 ### Community/Regional Resources

Resources in Blacksburg and the New River Valley.

1. Dedicated to issues of diversity, this office focuses on creating a diverse, inclusive campus community through its policies, the composition of students, faculty and staff, the curriculum, and additional services and programs.

2. Check out academic programs that focus on the study of culture, ethnicity, role, religion, and gender, including Africana Studies, American Indian Studies, Judaic Studies, Asian Area Studies, the Department of Religion and Culture, and Women's and Gender Studies.

3. Search the list of student clubs and organizations to find those that fit your interests and background, and learn about the multicultural programs and services offered.

4. Find out about supportive resources for the diverse populations on campus, including the Americans with Disabilities Act Services, Veterans Services and Information, Women's Center, Multicultural Center, Center for the Enhancement of Engineering Diversity, and the Black Cultural Center.

5. Learn about the broader town/city/regional resources available if you live and work off campus or if you're interested in connecting more fully with the surrounding community.

The purpose of these offices and committees is to raise awareness and educate students from all backgrounds about the diversity that is represented on campus; they also offer counseling and academic assistance. Some of these resources provide a safe space for students to meet others from similar backgrounds and to find support.

QUICK TIP

Build Connections

If you have minority status at your college, it's normal to experience feelings of loneliness or to wonder if you belong. Remember that clubs, associations, and campus resources dedicated to diversity can help you build a meaningful community that makes you feel more at home.

> ### ✓ CHECKLIST OF WAYS TO FIND SUPPORT AROUND DIFFERENCE
>
> ☐ Engage in activities that speak to your background, interests, and beliefs.
>
> ☐ Visit campus resources that are dedicated to issues of diversity.
>
> ☐ Find other campus resources that offer student support (for example, the Counseling Center, First-Year Programs Office, Advising Office, Student Services Office, or Disability Services Office).
>
> ☐ Take classes focused on issues of diversity to engage in meaningful conversations and to find others with similar interests.
>
> ☐ Talk to other students about their experiences with difference and how they found support.
>
> ☐ Find mentors on campus, and talk honestly with them about your experiences with diversity.

Learn from Differences

At the same time you're finding comfortable communities and building friendships on campus, recognize the value of learning from those who are different from you. An important goal for colleges and universities is to expose students to diverse experiences and environments. Many campuses want to push students outside their comfort zones by providing opportunities for interaction with people from various backgrounds and belief systems. Take advantage of this unique chance to expand your own understanding of others and to challenge whatever stereotypes and prejudices you have, either knowingly or unknowingly.

⑤ STRATEGIES TO BRIDGE DIFFERENCES

1. **Organize a study session.**

   When you meet up with classmates to study, share something about your background (religion, high school, culture) during the study session.

2. **Plan an outing or activity.**

   Organizing an activity around a common interest or goal is a way to meet people from different backgrounds.

3. **Share food that is traditional or special in your life.**

   Sharing a meal breaks the ice and is a fun way to connect with other people.

4. **Share pictures.**

   As the saying goes, "A picture is worth a thousand words." Use pictures to connect with others, and connect through Facebook, too.

5. **Open up about struggles you have experienced in your past and at college.**

   If you can share something important about your life, others will often follow suit, allowing for a meaningful connection.

Authentic Communication

The best way to explore diversity at your college is through communication. Don't be afraid to ask others about their lives and where they come from. Reciprocate by openly sharing information about yourself. Being able to communicate authentically tears down the barriers between people, which are often based on fear. Differences can create fear because we are often afraid of the unknown or the unfamiliar. By talking about what your family is like or describing your community, you can open up a dialogue in a relationship. While describing and noticing all the differences, you will probably notice similarities as well. This type of communication provides opportunities to connect deeply with someone else, helping to remove any awkwardness that may exist.

Mutual Respect

We all have a natural desire to connect with others and communicate comfortably. You may not become best friends with everyone you meet, but anything can happen when you make the effort to get to know someone. When you listen closely to other people—classmates, teammates, roommates, or advisors—and understand what experiences have shaped their lives, you'll be able to understand who they are and the differences they bring to the table. You won't always agree with them, but you will respect them. If mutual respect forms the basis of your relationships, you will go far.

 CASE STUDY

Corey describes his experiences around diversity and difference on campus.

My school is a microcosm of the real world. Various socioeconomic classes, racial and ethnic groups, gender identities, and religious beliefs are represented here. I am a member of Ujamaa, a student group for individuals who identify with or support the African diaspora and seek to raise cultural and social awareness on campus.

I have worked to find a community here, which hasn't always been easy. I have learned to ignore the stares; instead, I focus on people who will hear my words. I also work to bridge differences by speaking at every public forum I can. I host various programs on diversity that stress the importance of the African American (or African diasporic) presence on campus. Though it is sometimes difficult to see myself as a teacher, it is rewarding to see that my story has erased someone's ignorance and that my efforts have produced a meaningful alliance on campus that will help create change.

QUESTIONS FOR REFLECTION: Do you belong to an organization on campus that has made you feel more comfortable or more included? If so, how has your participation helped? If not, do you know of any clubs or associations you could join in the near future? Have you visited your school's diversity center to find out what supportive services are offered?

The social scene on college campuses varies widely depending on the size of the school, the location, whether the student population is primarily residential or commuter, the presence of fraternities and sororities, and rule enforcement. Whichever college you attend, you will be faced with decisions about the type of social life you'd like to engage in. Making smart decisions about socializing will help keep you safe.

Socializing in College

In college, you can find many ways to socialize. You may attend college-sponsored events such as concerts, shows, movies, lectures, or athletic events. Groups and clubs often organize activities on or off campus. And you might host or attend parties in a residence hall, at a location off campus, or in a fraternity or sorority house.

Make Smart Choices

If you choose to drink alcohol socially, you can make choices that will keep you healthy and safe.

Stick together. Attend a party with someone you trust. It's important to have one or more friends looking after you, just as you should be looking after them. Make a pact that you will stay connected in some way throughout the party and that you will leave together.

QUICK TIP

Communicate Clearly
Communicate clearly with your friends before you arrive at a party. Do you plan to stay for one hour or four hours? Will you stick together throughout the event? If you get separated, how will you find one another? Before you arrive at the party, understand each other's expectations so that both you and your friends can pick up on warning signs if necessary.

Know your limits.   Knowing your own limits with alcohol can be difficult, so it's important to always have at least one friend with you at a party. Agree to stop drinking or to go home together if one of you has hit a limit or whenever you feel out of control or over-whelmed. Have fun, but make each other's safety a priority.

Stay in control.   Always be aware of how much and how fast you are drinking. It's easy to get caught up in the party spirit and drink to excess before you realize you are doing so. Make an effort to understand your limits and stay aware of what's going on around you; check periodically to ensure that you can make it home (with a friend) without a problem.

QUICK TIP

Recognize the Patterns of Binge Drinking

Binge drinking elevates blood alcohol concentrations very quickly—generally after four drinks for women and five drinks for men in a span of just two hours.[1] Binge drinking is often associated with alcohol problems, including alcohol abuse and dependence, alcohol poisoning, injury, and even death. Get help if you can't control your binge drinking. It could save your life.

Don't drink and drive.   You have probably heard this advice many times before, but it is extremely important. Drinking while under the influence is very dangerous—for you, for any passengers in the car, for other drivers, for pedestrians—and can cause death and life-changing injuries. If you have been drinking, especially if you are drunk, you will not be able to operate a vehicle safely. Even if you think you're okay, don't take the risk. It's not worth it.

---

[1] NIAAA, April 2012, 1.

QUICK TIP

Find a Safe Ride

If you're not sure you can get home safely, find someone else to drive you. Many campuses offer safe rides home by calling campus police, campus security, or campus safety. You might also be able to call a local phone number that is designated for safe rides home (be sure to program it in your phone!).

Consequences of Drinking

Social life at college can be a lot of fun, but drinking to excess can have negative ramifications for you and your future. Sadly, almost 2,000 college students between the ages of eighteen and twenty-four die each year from alcohol-related injuries (including vehicle crashes), almost 600,000 are injured while under the influence of alcohol, and almost 700,000 are assaulted by another student who has been drinking.[2] This information is not intended to scare you; rather, it's important to know what can happen when drinking gets out of control.

Academic consequences. No doubt you have heard the saying "Work hard and play hard." Some college students are able to live by this motto. Many students, though, find that too much partying leads to lower academic performance, for a variety of reasons. You may find that partying interferes with the time needed to engage in academics. Drinking and drugs can lead to sleep disturbances and many other health issues, making it harder to concentrate on assignments and tests and during lectures. In fact, one-quarter of college students report that they have experienced academic consequences resulting from drinking—including lower grades and missed classes.[3]

---

[2] Ibid., 1.
[3] Ibid., 2.

Alcohol poisoning. Many students don't know their own limits when it comes to drinking, especially if the drinks are being mixed by others. Drinking too much too fast is common, especially if you feel pressured to do so. Drinking to excess can lead to alcohol poisoning, a serious condition that usually requires emergency hospitalization and can even be deadly.

Alcohol dependence. Many college students become dependent on alcohol; in fact, almost 20 percent of young people between the ages of eighteen and twenty-four suffer from alcohol addiction. Sadly, only 5 percent seek treatment.[4] If you find that you drink more than you intend to or for longer periods of time; suffer from withdrawal symptoms; spend a lot of time seeking out alcohol and give up other normal activities; and try to cut down on your drinking to no avail, you may be showing signs of alcohol dependence. Reaching out for help may be scary, but it could save your future and even your life. You don't have to suffer alone. Talk to someone at the student support center, counseling office, or health center.

Legal trouble. Alcohol may be easy to obtain at college, but if you're under twenty-one, it is still illegal. If you get caught by campus police, town or city police, or campus staff, you could be put on probation, expelled, or even jailed. Each college has a different policy on underage drinking, so be sure you're fully aware of what your college's policy is. If you decide to take risks, be sure you understand the consequences you might face. Although you may feel invincible in college, you can make one big mistake that could have a significant impact on your future.

Drug Abuse

Like drinking, using illicit drugs is often part of the college social scene. And like drinking, doing drugs is both dangerous and risky. Depending on the type of drug, illicit drugs can produce side effects such as drowsiness, disorientation, increased heart rate,

---

[4] Ibid., 2.

---

⑤ SMART THINGS TO DO IF YOU'VE HAD TOO MUCH TO DRINK

1. **Stop drinking alcohol and start drinking water.**

   Water will help with the dehydration associated with drinking alcohol.

2. **Don't drive a car under any circumstances.**

   Stay where you are until you are sober, get a ride from a designated driver, or call campus police/security/safety for a safe ride home.

3. **Stay put if you feel you can't walk home.**

   Don't take a risk and try to walk anywhere if you are drunk. Stay put and call for a safe ride home, or leave with a friend who can get you home safely.

4. **If you are scared or feeling sick, call campus police or 911 immediately.**

   Your health and well-being are more important than any possible consequences.

5. **If you find yourself drinking too much too often, get help.**

   Talk to a campus counselor, your advisor, a mentor, or a friend, and be honest about what's happening.

---

delusions, and hallucinations. A drug overdose can lead to convulsions, coma, or even death. And because almost 13 percent of young people eighteen to twenty-five drive while under the influence of illicit drugs, there are serious risks to others.[5]

Consequences.   Other serious consequences can arise from drug abuse. Your academic life will suffer if drugs become a significant focus of your time, especially if you experience withdrawal symptoms ranging from tremors, cramps, and irritability to anxiety and depression.[6] Your future could also be in jeopardy if you get caught.

---

[5] US Department of Health and Human Services, 2010 National Survey on Drug Use and Health Results.

[6] Mayo Foundation for Medical Education and Research, Drug Addiction, "Treatments and Drug," Oct. 1, 2011, http://www .mayoclinic.com/health/drug-addiction/DS00183/DSECTION =treatments-and-drugs.

Possession of illegal drugs, like underage drinking, can lead to probation, expulsion, and arrest.

Addiction.   Use of illegal drugs can also lead to drug addiction, a compulsive need to use drugs on a regular basis in order to function normally. Addiction is a serious disease that can cause problems in all aspects of your life—harming your relationships, academics, work life, and health. Watch for the signs of addiction, such as neglecting your responsibilities as a student and at work, fighting more than normal, engaging in risky behavior, and avoiding activities you used to enjoy.[7] Seek help. If you find that your life revolves around drugs, even though you know they are hurting you, seek help. Staff at your college's counseling office, health clinic, or student support center want to help. If friends or others you trust on campus reach out and urge you to get help, listen to them. They have your best interests at heart.

 CASE STUDY

Marcus shares his thoughts on managing his social life at college.

> My best advice is to stay true to yourself. There will definitely be drugs and alcohol in college, along with pressures to indulge. Always be mindful of your limits, and make sure the choices that you make are *yours*. Ask yourself, "Do I really want to be drinking this right now?" It's crucial to check in with yourself. No one knows your limits better than you do. Listen to yourself. You will face some external pressures, but it's up to you either to buy into those pressures or to ignore them. Don't be afraid to speak to your friends, family, and mentors to help you make these choices.

---

[7] Ibid., "Symptoms."

At the same time, know that you can have an amazing social life without drugs or alcohol. Many people at college don't drink or do drugs, or they do so in moderation. And you can find plenty of ways to have fun with your friends—movies, games, concerts, plays, dancing, restaurants, and so on—that don't involve alcohol or drugs.

When I first came to college, I had a hard time finding a balance between my social life and my academics. The best way to find this balance is to be realistic with yourself and to be aware of how you're feeling. For example, if you're sick of doing a reading or problem set for class, it might be time to take a breather, so call a few friends and do something relaxing for a short while. And it's important to have fun on the weekends in order to give your mind a real break. But you also need to be mindful of your academics because you are at college to learn. Try to find a balance that works for you.

QUESTIONS FOR REFLECTION: Have you ever felt pressure to socialize in ways that are uncomfortable for you? Have you thought about strategies to have fun, while staying true to yourself? If you're having difficulty doing this, be honest with someone you trust—a mentor, an advisor, a college counselor, a family member, or a friend. The more you can open up, the more likely you'll be able to figure out and follow through on what's most comfortable for you in your social life.

Sexual Assault

Sexual assault is a serious problem that frequently occurs when people drink to excess, although it sometimes happens even without the presence of alcohol. An estimated 97,000 students between the ages of eighteen and twenty-four are victims of alcohol-related sexual assault or date rape each year.[8] When you drink, you become less inhibited, and when you drink to excess, you may not fully be aware of what you're doing or may become helpless to stop uncomfortable or unwanted behavior.

Be Aware and Alert

Whether you're on a date or meet someone at a party, be clear about your expectations when it comes to sexual activity. What behavior is and is not okay? And if your partner won't listen to your requests, leave as soon as you start to feel uncomfortable. If that isn't possible, try to get help. It's a good idea to bring friends with you to a party—let them know that you need help or tell them that it's time to leave together.

Watch Your Drink

Quite often, drugs called "date-rape drugs" are slipped into drinks surreptitiously. These drugs can cause victims to become mentally and physically incapacitated, making it difficult, if not impossible, to talk coherently or to move their body. In these terrible circumstances, victims are helpless to defend themselves if they are sexually assaulted; afterward, they may not be aware of what has happened. To stay safe, make or pour your own drink, and keep it in view at all times. If you put the drink down for a while, don't hesitate to get a new one. You don't want to take any risks with your safety.

Get Help

If you find yourself in a situation where you feel powerless to stop what's happening and are personally violated against your wishes, you must get help immediately. Many schools have sexual assault offices with twenty-four-hour hotlines staffed by trained counselors who are

---

[8] NIAAA, April 2012, 1.

ready to help. Program that hotline number—as well as the numbers of the campus police and college health clinic—into your cell phone. When you call the hotline, a counselor will help you figure out where to go and what to do. If your school does not have a hotline, call or walk to the campus police or the health clinic. To obtain the support and assistance you need, you must talk to a trained professional immediately.

QUICK TIP

Stay Safe

Know the locations of all the safety phones on your campus. They usually have a blue light above them and therefore are sometimes called "blue light" phones. Use one whenever you feel unsafe or in the case of an emergency.

CHECKLIST FOR STAYING SOCIALLY SAFE ON CAMPUS

- ☐ Go to parties with friends and leave with them.
- ☐ Check in with friends throughout the party.
- ☐ Tell someone if you are drinking for the first time or are drinking more than normal.
- ☐ If you feel uncomfortable or overwhelmed at a party, leave.
- ☐ If you've had too much to drink and are scared, get help from a friend or call campus police or 911.
- ☐ If you are going out with someone you don't know well, tell a friend where you are going and when you expect to return.
- ☐ Be aware of the locations of blue-light phones in case of an emergency.
- ☐ Program into your cell phone the numbers for campus police/security/safety, for safe rides home, and for the campus health clinic.

Protecting Your Privacy

Take time to understand the privacy options on Facebook. Be sure that only people you're comfortable with can find you on Facebook and can view the photos and information you post. However, regardless of your own privacy settings, others can post photos and information about you to their own pages. Be sensible about what you post, and know what you can do to manage your Facebook account.

facebook

⌂ **Help Center** ▸ **Privacy**

1 Basics >

2 Controlling Who Can Find You >

3 Troubleshoot Privacy Issues

Accessing Your Facebook Data

Minors & Privacy

4 Safety >

Cookies, Pixels & Similar Technologies

5 Questions About Our Privacy Policy

External Resources

Back ↩

1 Learn about the basic privacy settings and tools, including how you can select an audience for items you post, who can send friend requests, how you can stop people from posting on your timeline, and what happens to your personal information after it is deleted.

2. Control who can send you friend requests, and find out how to block someone from starting a conversation or seeing your timeline posts. Also learn how your information will be viewed in search engine results.

3. If privacy issues come up or your privacy settings aren't working, be sure to troubleshoot the problem by reading about solutions online at the Facebook Help Center or by contacting Facebook.

4. Read about safety tips, including adjusting your privacy setting, blocking users who send inappropriate communication, and reporting abusive language on the site. You can also find safety resources if you become concerned about someone on Facebook who discusses substance abuse or suicide.

5. Take the time to read and understand Facebook's privacy policy, including how you can access personal information on Facebook, and what you can do if you have a privacy complaint.

Although the topic of sexual assault isn't an easy one, it's important to address this issue because sexual assault is more prevalent on college campuses than reported. Generally, you're quite safe at college, but you'll be even safer if you know what to do in different situations. It is also your responsibility to look out for your friends; if you understand what to do in an emergency and how to get help when necessary, you'll be helping those you care about most.

Social Media

You might be wondering what information on social media is doing in a chapter about being socially smart. The Internet is an integral part of social life for most of us, especially students, but, sadly, the Internet isn't always a friendly place. Given the number of people who can access the information you post to social media sites, you can't possibly know the intentions of every person who views your photos, status updates, and personal information. Be careful when you post personal information online. You may think that only friends and family can view your information, but that may not be the case. Your privacy settings won't always protect you, so assume that almost anyone can and will see what you've posted. For example, if you allow friends of friends to view the information on your Facebook page, you don't really know who those "friends of friends" might be.

Consider Your Safety

On the Internet, it is easy to find and exchange information. If you ever feel as though your safety is at risk—if you have received offensive, violent, or abusive messages, or if you feel that someone you are connected to online is crossing boundaries—talk immediately to an instructor, an advisor, a counselor, or a security person at your college. A boundary violation can be something as simple as someone writing on your wall, posting a picture with a label, or texting in a way that just doesn't feel right. Don't ignore your gut feeling, because your gut is usually right.

Deleting Is Difficult

As you use technology in college, remember that the words you type and the pictures you post—whether via e-mail or on Facebook or Twitter—are easy to share with others and difficult to delete. Be smart about what you post online. Assume that anyone—including employers and college officials—can see what's on your Facebook profile. Do you really want the pictures you just posted to be seen by your college advisor? By the company that just interviewed you for the summer internship of your dreams? Your reputation, college status, job opportunities, and admission to graduate school are on

Since college admissions officers might see his Facebook page, Mike used Photoshop to erase the beer cans in his hands, replacing them with books.

▲

Facebook is a great way to share photos and memories with others. Just remember that you probably shouldn't let certain people see some of your photos or posts. Use Facebook privacy settings, and most important, use good judgment.

the line, so remember: nothing is completely private online.

Recognize Stress

Social media sites can be stress relievers, but sometimes they can also be a source of stress. When you are working on a difficult class reading or a particularly tough economics problem set, you might take a much-needed break by visiting a social media site. You might even need to use social media as part of your course work if your class has a Facebook page or if the instructor relays information through Twitter. However, if you spend so much time on these sites that you can't finish the class reading or can't concentrate fully on the problem set, you can become quite stressed. Find ways for Facebook and other Internet sites to enhance, rather than impede, your studying.

Managing
Your Money

Managing your money is one of the many responsibilities you'll have as a college student and one of the most important life skills you can develop. You may already have experience with a budget, a bank account, and credit cards, or college might be the first time you're dealing with your own finances. Either way, college is a good time to learn how to manage your finances, which will help to ensure your long-term financial health.

Create and Manage a Budget

The first step when managing your money in college is assessing your overall financial situation. Start by determining your sources of income. Do you have money saved for college? Are you receiving financial aid in the form of loans, stipends, or scholarships? Are you working, or do you plan to get a job while in school? Estimate how much money you will receive each week or each month from all of these sources. Next, calculate the expenses you'll likely have throughout the year—books, food, housing, commuting, clothes, activities, and so on.

Once you have determined this information, create a grid that breaks down the term into blocks of time (weekly or monthly). Then, put together a simple budget that lists how much money you have saved, how much money you will receive and expect to earn, and your estimated expenses.

Keeping track of your expenses may sound simple, but it's easy to lose track of what you're spending when you're busy with classes, studying, activities, a job, and various other commitments. Make it a priority to determine a budgeting system that works for you. To stay within your budget, do you need to review it every week? Or can you manage by checking your budget just once a month? Whatever system you prefer, add it to your calendar so that your budget doesn't get lost in the shuffle.

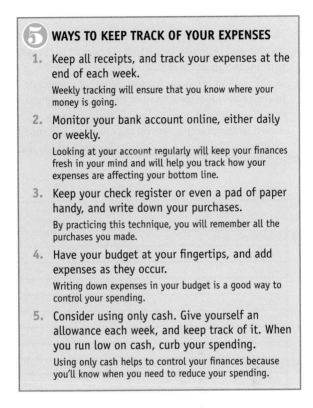

⑤ WAYS TO KEEP TRACK OF YOUR EXPENSES

1. Keep all receipts, and track your expenses at the end of each week.

   Weekly tracking will ensure that you know where your money is going.

2. Monitor your bank account online, either daily or weekly.

   Looking at your account regularly will keep your finances fresh in your mind and will help you track how your expenses are affecting your bottom line.

3. Keep your check register or even a pad of paper handy, and write down your purchases.

   By practicing this technique, you will remember all the purchases you made.

4. Have your budget at your fingertips, and add expenses as they occur.

   Writing down expenses in your budget is a good way to control your spending.

5. Consider using only cash. Give yourself an allowance each week, and keep track of it. When you run low on cash, curb your spending.

   Using only cash helps to control your finances because you'll know when you need to reduce your spending.

Understand Your Financial Aid Package

A critical piece of your financial situation is your financial aid package. You may have received a combination of federal loans, grants, scholarships, stipends, and work-study to help with tuition and other expenses. If you have any questions about your financial aid in the short or long term, meet with your financial aid officer as soon as possible to be sure you fully understand your aid package.

Visual Walkthrough

Budgeting

The following example of a monthly budget lists income and expenses by category. Feel free to format your budget in any way that works for you. You might want to break the budget down into weeks or to create a budget for a term or the whole academic year. You may not need to use all the categories shown in the example, or you may need to add some categories. The more you personalize the budget, the more likely you'll be to use it.

	Budgeted Amount	Actual Amount
① Sources of Income		
Job(s)		
Savings		
Loans		
Grants/scholarships		
Other		
Total Income		
② Expenses		
Tuition		
⑤ Household		
Rent/mortgage/room and board		
Utilities (electricity, gas, cable, Internet)		
Child care		
Cell phone		
Food		
Groceries		
Eating out		
Transportation		
Car payment and insurance		
Gas and repairs		
Bus/subway pass		
Books and supplies		
Entertainment		
Movies		
Concerts		
Campus events		

The column headers are marked ③ Budgeted Amount and ④ Actual Amount.

	Budgeted Amount	Actual Amount
Miscellaneous		
Clothing		
Household products		
Other		
6 Total Expenses		

1. List all the sources of your income for each month. Include any income from a job (part-time, full-time, summer, internship); savings and money from family; loans; and grants, scholarships, or stipend payments. Your financial aid statement may provide aid information for an entire term, so you need to calculate the amount of your aid for each month. Talk to a financial aid officer if you need help with this.

2. For each month, list the nature of your expenses, including tuition, household items, phone, food, transportation, books, supplies, entertainment, and other miscellaneous items you'll need.

3. List your budgeted estimate for both income and expenses. Try to keep your expenses lower than your income so that you live within your means and don't run out of money or go into debt.

4. Keep track of your actual income and expenses. For example, if your job hours increase, so will your job income. And keeping track of your actual expenses will help you stay within your budget. If you have to pay more for books than you expected, you might need to cut down on entertainment or clothing purchases to stay within your budget.

5. Break down broad expense categories into more specific items so that you know exactly where your money goes.

6. To fully understand your financial situation each month, total up your expenses and compare your expenses to your total income. If you're struggling to live within your means, you have to either cut back on spending or find some way to increase your income. Talk to a financial aid officer or a college advisor if you need assistance.

Types of Aid

Your financial aid package may include various types of aid, such as aid from your college, from the state government or the federal government, and from nonprofit and private organizations. Take time to understand each line item on your financial aid statement, which might include any of the following categories of aid.

Loans. A number of loan options, including federal loans and private loans, are available to help pay for college. A loan is money that you borrow and will eventually have to pay back with interest. Federal loans include Direct Subsidized Loans (for students with financial need), Direct Unsubsidized Loans (for students with no requirement to demonstrate need), PLUS Loans (for parents of dependent students to help pay education expenses), and Federal Perkins Loans (for students with exceptional financial need). Private loans come from a lender such as a bank or credit union.

Federal loans have a fixed interest rate that is usually lower than private loan interest rates. Private loans sometimes have variable interest rates, meaning that the rate can rise and fall depending on the terms of the loan; variable interest rates create more uncertainty as to your future payments. The cost of a private loan may also depend on your credit score and other factors, and you may not be able to get a private loan without an established credit history. However, federal loans (except for PLUS Loans) do not require a credit history and can actually help you develop a good credit history if you manage your payments well.

Federal and private loans have different repayment plans. You do not need to repay federal loans until after you graduate, leave school, or enroll less than half time. However, you usually have to repay private loans while you are still in school, and you have to pay all the interest that accrues during college (and thereafter). By contrast, if you have a federal *subsidized* loan, the government, not you, pays the interest that accrues during college.

Grants. Grant money is aid that is given to you to help cover the cost of college and does not need to be repaid. Many types of grants are available, and they can come from the federal government, the state government, your college or university, and public and private organizations. Federal Pell Grants are awarded to students who demonstrate financial need, and grants from your college also are usually based on financial need.

Scholarships. A scholarship, like a grant, is money that you do not need to pay back. Scholarships are awarded to students based on various criteria that reflect the values or priorities of the awarding body. Colleges, as well as high schools and state governments, often award merit scholarships based on high achievement. Some organizations offer scholarships with eligibility requirements such as race, ethnicity, religion, college major, or location. Online, you can find a variety of college scholarships by Googling "college scholarships." Although the sheer number of scholarships available might feel overwhelming, make the effort to apply—you might be able to find additional money to help defray the cost of college.

Work-study. If you can demonstrate financial need, you might be eligible for federal work-study jobs that provide part-time work opportunities that help cover the cost of college. Schools that participate in the Federal Work-Study Program offer work-study jobs that can be on or off campus, depending on how the school administers the program. Work-study jobs are often related to a student's course of study and community service work.

Stipends. Some students receive a stipend, or an "award," which is usually a one-time payment to help offset the cost of attending college. Besides tuition, college students have additional expenses such as food, clothes, and transportation; to help students pay for these expenses, some colleges include stipends in financial aid packages, usually for students with financial need. Stipends can reduce the hours you might otherwise need to work to make ends meet.

Applying for Aid

To help your school determine what your financial aid package will include, you need to complete financial aid applications. Colleges will ask you to fill out the Free Application for Federal Student Aid (FAFSA); some colleges will also ask you to fill out the College Scholarship Service (CSS) Profile. Even if you don't think you will receive financial aid, be sure to fill out all the aid applications so that your school has a complete picture of your financial situation and can award appropriate levels of loans, grants, and scholarships.

Fill out the FAFSA. To be eligible for federal grants, loans, and work-study, you must fill out the FAFSA. This free application provides necessary financial information about you and your family that gives the college a clear idea of your ability to pay. Based on the cost of attending the school and the information you provide on the FAFSA, the college will determine how much money you receive in grants and scholarships, how much money you can borrow, and how much work-study you are eligible for. The FAFSA Web site (www.fafsa.ed.gov) provides more detailed information, including FAFSA deadlines, options for filing the FAFSA, and how to create a FAFSA PIN that will allow you to sign your forms online.

Complete a CSS Profile. You can find the CSS Profile, another financial aid form, on the College Board Web site (http://student.collegeboard.org/css-financial-aid -profile). More than 350 schools require students to submit the CSS Profile when they apply for financial aid. There is a fee for submitting a CSS Profile, but the fee is waived for students with financial need. The CSS Profile gathers additional financial information, more detailed than the FAFSA, to help colleges award institutional aid, including grants, scholarships, and loans.

Reapply each year. You need to reapply for financial aid every year that you attend college, so be aware of your college's financial aid application deadlines. Applying for aid each year is necessary because your financial aid package might need to be modified if your financial situation has changed, and colleges might need to alter the financial aid they can offer depending on changing institutional priorities or realities.

Use Credit Cards Wisely

The decision to obtain a credit card is an important one. As soon as you open a credit card, you start building a credit history, which is a good thing if you use the card wisely. All too often, though, credit cards tempt people to live beyond their means and to rack up debt that will negatively affect their credit score (and bank account). Because of the possible risks of using credit cards, you need to be fully informed before you decide to obtain one.

Choosing a Credit Card

Look for a credit card with no annual fee. Find out exactly how much interest will be charged if you do not pay your balance in full each month. Be aware of when interest starts accruing. Interest should accrue only if you do not pay the full balance on your monthly statement, not as soon as you make purchases. Credit cards often charge fees for missed or late payments, so know when your payment is due. Make sure you read all the literature accompanying the application. Late fees can be costly, and several late payments can negatively affect your credit score.

"I know my grades weren't that good, but on the plus side, I'm the only person in my dorm who hasn't maxed out a credit card."

▲

When you use a credit card, it's easy to lose sight of what you're spending. Even small purchases can really add up. Make an effort to keep track of your spending so that you reduce money stress!

Control Your Spending

Credit cards sometimes tempt people to overspend. Although credit cards are a convenient way to pay for things, and good to have in case of an emergency, you can quickly get into debt if you spend more than you have. If you can't pay off your credit card in full each month, you have to pay interest on the balance, which means you will pay more for each item you purchase. Credit card debt can quickly spiral out of control, especially if interest continues to accrue each month, making it harder and harder to pay off the credit card balance.

Know When to Put the Card Away

If you can't control your spending and can't pay off your credit card, stop using it. Think about switching to a bank debit card, which draws money directly from your checking account, or a prepaid credit card, which you load with a certain amount of money and can use until the money runs out. Using a prepaid credit card guarantees that you won't spend money you don't have.

Get Help

Be sure to talk to someone if you're having trouble making credit card payments, can't seem to stay within your budget, or feel overwhelmed financially. Your financial aid officer, your advisor, a mentor, or someone at the Student Services Center will be able to assist you or can direct you to other helpful campus resources. Managing your finances takes a lot of practice. Don't be afraid to ask questions and get help as soon as you need it.

✓ **CREDIT CARD APPLICATION CHECKLIST**

☐ Find a card with no annual fee.

☐ Understand how much interest you will be charged if you don't pay the full amount on your credit card each month.

☐ Make sure you are not being charged interest on items as soon as you buy them.

☐ Understand all fees and penalties for missed or late payments.

Your Credit History

Your credit history is *very* important, both now and in the future. It will influence your ability to borrow money from banks, buy a car, and get a mortgage for a house. Try to avoid negative strikes on your credit history. Pay off your credit cards in full each month; don't waste your money on interest and fees. If you can't afford a certain purchase, wait until you can. Staying in control of your personal finances will significantly reduce your stress and anxiety. And creating a budget will make you more aware of when you should and should not spend money.

How you handle your credit cards has a significant impact on your credit history, so be sure that you fully understand the terms of your credit cards and use them wisely. How you manage your checking account also influences your credit history. For example, if you bounce a check (that is, write a check without sufficient funds in your account), your credit history will be negatively affected. But if you keep close tabs on your spending and write down all purchases and payments, you will be on your way to maintaining a good credit history.

QUICK TIP

Live within Your Means

Strive to live within your means, even if you have to make sacrifices that others don't have to make. Living within your means isn't always easy, but it will help you in the long term, especially if you keep your credit history strong.

Taking the time to understand where you stand financially will be time well spent. And remember, if you need help figuring out how to manage your money, ask someone you trust. It's easy to run into financial trouble. The solution is to immediately address any financial problems so that they don't spiral out of control. Be proactive—you won't regret it.

 CASE STUDY

Bill shares his perspective on how to manage finances during college.

I had a work-study job three out of the four years I was in college. In my first year, I didn't have any system for managing my money. That changed when I had to cut back my job hours. I knew I needed to be more careful with my money. I learned more about budgeting by talking to my mentor, and I said no to things that weren't budget-friendly. I knew that if I didn't practice budgeting in college, I was going to have a hard time when I entered the working world.

I do have a credit card, but I can use it only for food and gas, which is great because I'm not tempted to spend it on clothes or shoes. I have been pretty good at paying it off. However, I do have a balance now that I'm trying to pay off, which has been stressful.

QUESTIONS FOR REFLECTION: Have you figured out a budgeting system to keep track of your finances? If so, does it help you keep your credit card payments under control? If not, do you have any attitudes about money that prevent you from putting together a budget?

Chapter 15
What's Next?

A lot happens in your first year of college. You meet classmates, learn about campus resources and support systems, get to know your advisor, choose a mentor, figure out an academic plan, hone college study skills, engage in social life, and manage your money. And as you move through your remaining years of college, you'll have even more to think about.

Dig into Your Major

Once you choose your major, you will spend the next several terms until graduation digging deep into the subject matter. In your major field of study, you will be required to take courses that will help you become an expert in the discipline you've chosen. Be sure you take these courses when you need to. Continue to put together an academic plan that fulfills requirements in a timely way, and remember the importance of a balanced course load. And when you are allowed to choose electives within your major, try to find classes that are particularly interesting and, if possible, that fit your learning preferences.

QUICK TIP

Develop a Manageable Academic Plan

If you plan to minor in a subject or to take a double major, be aware of all the requirements you'll need to fulfill, and meet with your advisor to develop an academic plan that fulfills your goals and is manageable.

A New Advisor

Once you declare a major, you will probably be assigned a new advisor who works within that discipline. Use your new advisor as a trusted resource when you need to make decisions about academics or when other questions and issues arise. It's also a good idea to stay in touch with your old advisor and to update him or her on your life as you progress through college.

Writing a Thesis

Your college might offer you the opportunity to complete a thesis (an in-depth study of a topic of your choosing, related to your major) before you graduate. You might write a thesis for a number of reasons. Sometimes a thesis is required for certain majors or to graduate with honors. Or you might become interested in a topic within your major and want to spend a great deal of time researching and writing about it. Thesis requirements vary from college to college, but usually you will earn credits while writing a thesis; therefore, you will not take a full course load at the same time.

> ### QUICK TIP
>
> ### *Graduate with Honors*
> If you are interested in graduating with honors, find out what your college's eligibility requirements are. Usually, you need an exceptional grade point average as well as high marks on a thesis. Most colleges offer honors in the form of *cum laude* ("with honor"), *magna cum laude* ("with great honor"), and *summa cum laude* ("with highest honor").

Writing a thesis is a big undertaking, but it can also be extremely rewarding, especially if you find a topic you're passionate about. If you are interested in writing a thesis, you'll need to determine the topic you want to study, approximately a year before it's due. This is so that you have enough time to conduct any required research. Your department will have guidelines about what topics are appropriate and will help you find a thesis advisor who will advise you solely on your thesis (you will keep your regular advisor as well). Your thesis advisor needs to approve your topic and the scope of the project. You will meet with your thesis advisor regularly, especially as you complete drafts for review.

QUICK TIP

Write a Thesis

Once you pick a major, you might start thinking about writing a thesis (even though it may be several terms in the future). Talk to your regular advisor to fully understand what is required and how you might fit thesis research and writing into your long-term academic plan.

Practice Study Skills

Study skills are relevant throughout college and remain useful after you obtain a degree. You'll find that the more you practice time management, note-taking, reading strategies, paper writing, critical thinking, studying, and test-taking, the more successful you'll be as a student. These skills take some effort to master, but, with practice, you can make them part of your regular routine.

Ask Periodically: Are the Strategies Working?

Determining the best study strategies for you requires some trial and error. Some strategies may work better than others, depending on your preferences and learning style. After your first year, assess whether you've figured out a method of taking notes that makes it easy to study from them and to follow up with instructors if you have questions. Do you take different types of notes depending on the subject of the class? If not, why? Do you think you might perform better on exams if you try out a few different note-taking strategies?

Similarly, are the strategies you're using to understand class readings effective? If you end up having to reread everything before a test, think about what isn't working. Are you skimming too much or highlighting more than you should, making it more difficult to pull out the main idea and important details? Are you writing marginal notes as you read?

And what about your strategies for time management? Is your planner system working for you? Are you staying on top of your assignments and tests, and do you start them in advance so that you're not cramming the night before? If not, try noting in your planner when you should begin assignments and start studying for tests, as a way to push yourself to get going ahead of time. Are you still struggling with procrastination? If so, try breaking down your work into manageable chunks and scheduling rejuvenating breaks, two techniques that will make you more productive.

Take time to reflect on your critical thinking skills, too. Is it becoming easier to engage in this type of deeper thinking when you do readings, write papers, and take notes? If you're still having trouble or find that your instructors expect more critical thinking, revisit the five steps for critical thinking in Chapter 4: ask questions, evaluate your own reactions, analyze what might be missing, make connections while looking at the bigger picture, and apply the material to your own life experiences.

An important part of college life is studying and test-taking. Have you become more comfortable with college test situations? Have you been getting good grades on your tests? If your grades aren't what you expected given the amount of time you studied, are you memorizing concepts, rather than deeply understanding them? Try to take study notes in your own words that condense material into meaningful chunks. Would visual representations of material help your understanding? And what about the actual test? Are you struggling to finish? If so, remember to pace yourself. Is test anxiety a problem for you? If you're blanking, consider freewriting to get your mind flowing on the topic at hand. If test anxiety persists, be sure to talk to someone in your school's Academic Advising Office or counseling center.

Are you having any difficulty writing papers? If you get stuck, remember to use freewriting as a way to get you moving on writing assignments. Have you asked others to look over your papers, or do you usually write them on your own? Do you think your writing process works? If not, use the college's writing center, and talk with your instructor well before the due date to be sure you're on the right track. Writing a few rough drafts can improve the final product.

Don't Hesitate to Get Help

If you find that you're struggling in your classes and that the study strategies offered in this book don't help much, take the initiative and seek additional assistance from your instructors, your advisor, the Academic Advising Office, or the counseling center on campus. It can be frustrating to work hard but still not do well academically. Tap into all the resources your school offers to get on track for success.

Figure Out Your Future

After (and probably during) your first year, you'll probably start thinking about your future. Maybe you've chosen a major that sets you on a specific career path, or maybe you're studying something you love but are still uncertain about what career you'll pursue after you graduate. Both scenarios are normal, and both require the assistance of experts.

Use the Career Services Office

Your college's Career Services Office can help you make decisions about your future career. Be sure to meet with the counselors there; they can help you evaluate all the career paths available to you and the many job possibilities within those careers. With a counselor's guidance, you can think more carefully about relevant factors that could influence your career and job decisions.

Potential employers will notice errors on written correspondence, no matter how trivial. Take the time to thoroughly edit and proofread everything you send so that employers will focus on your experience and skills, not on careless mistakes.

Negotiate a Job Offer

Not only can career counselors help you explore career options, but they can also help you negotiate a job offer when the time comes. For a good frame of reference, ask for a counselor's perspective on salary expectations and benefit packages within the field.

Work on your résumé. When you apply for summer positions, internships, and jobs after graduation, you'll need to submit a résumé and a cover letter. For help in preparing these two documents, meet with a career counselor to be sure you have included all the necessary information, formatted the documents properly, and caught any grammatical or spelling errors. Remember: your résumé and cover letter will be the first impression potential employers get of you.

Tap into Resources
Career offices usually publish a number of resource materials—in print and online—that provide advice on preparing résumés and cover letters, conducting informational interviews, searching for a job, interviewing with potential employers, and applying to graduate schools.

Engage in mock interviews. Once you send out your résumé and cover letter, an employer might ask you to come in for an interview. Practicing for interviews will put you more at ease during the actual interview. Find out if the Career Services Office provides opportunities to engage in mock interviews. Working with a career counselor on interview techniques will help you understand what skills are important to employers and how you can best highlight your strengths and interest in the position.

Use Alumni and Recruiting Resources

Career counselors aren't the only ones who can offer you valuable career advice. College alumni can provide insight into career fields they have pursued and may be able to help you with job searches in those fields. If the Career Services Office has a list of alumni willing to speak to college students, take advantage of this resource. The Career Services Office might also offer recruiting opportunities during which employers come to the campus to meet with students at a job fair. These employers usually have open positions students can apply for. Find out when your campus will be hosting a job fair and how to engage in the process.

Visual Walkthrough

Résumé Writing

Your résumé provides an overview of your skills, accomplishments, experience, and interests. It takes some effort to put together a résumé that employers will notice. Be sure to take the time necessary to create a résumé that is thorough, easy to read, concise, organized, and interesting and that highlights your strengths. And remember to use the counselors at the Career Services Office—they can help you determine what information should be included in your résumé and can also offer feedback on what changes might improve your résumé.

1. Include your contact information on your résumé so that potential employers know how to reach you.

2. Put your education information at the top of your résumé, and add important academic details to highlight your academic interests and accomplishments.

3. Include sections that describe your work and volunteer experience, as well as any significant activities, in order to give employers an idea of your skills, expertise, and interests.

4. To create a fuller picture of yourself, add a section that highlights your skills and interests.

5. Include dates on your résumé because employers want to know when your experiences took place and how long you engaged in them. List items in reverse chronological order, putting your most recent experiences at the top of each section.

6. Add succinct details about your experience and activities to demonstrate your accomplishments, responsibilities, skills, and leadership.

Kevin Nathans

1-555-321-1234 • E-mail: kevin.nathans@email.com ①
123 Main Street, East Lansing, MI 42524

EDUCATION ②

Michigan State University (MSU), College of Engineering
East Lansing, MI　　　　　　　**Expect to graduate May 2015**
B.A. in Civil Engineering. Additional course work in Computer Science and
Spanish.

Farmington High School, Farmington, MI　　**Graduated June 2011**
Achievements: National Honor Society, Senior Class Treasurer, Science
Honor Society President, Soccer Team Captain.

WORK/VOLUNTEER EXPERIENCE ③

Department of Computer Science and Engineering, MSU,
East Lansing, MI　　　　　　　**September 2012–Present** ⑤
Research Assistant in Games for Entertainment and Learning Lab
- Devote 6–8 hours a week to research focused on innovative and
educational digital games.
- Train in research methods and 3-D computer science gaming methods.

MSU Alternative Spring Break, New Orleans, LA　　**March 2013**
Team Leader
- Organized Habitat for Humanity volunteer experience for 30 participants ⑥
as an alternative spring break option.
- Led a team of 10 on-site in New Orleans and completed the paint job
throughout the two-story house.

State Farm Insurance, Livonia, MI　　　　　　**Summer 2012**
Claims Assistant
- Responded to inquiries about the status of insurance claims and worked
closely with managers to process claims.
- Reorganized computer system in office to increase efficiency and improve
electronic communication.

ACTIVITIES ③

MSU American Society of Civil Engineers,
East Lansing, MI　　　　　　　**November 2012–Present**
Treasurer
- Oversee funds for campus events and help organize yearly conferences for
the Michigan engineering community.

MSU Ultimate Frisbee Club Team,
East Lansing, MI　　　　　　　**September 2011–Present**
Co-captain
- Run practices for teammates, schedule competition with other colleges,
play in games regularly.

MSU Student Government Academic Assembly,
East Lansing, MI　　　　　　　**September 2011–May 2012**
First-Year Representative
- Contributed to meetings focused on academic policies and tuition issues.
Communicated any changes to first-year classmates.

SKILLS & INTERESTS ④

- Languages: Spanish (fluent), French (proficient).
- Computer Skills: Advanced programming in C++, experience with Excel
and Powerpoint.
- Interests: Hiking, soccer, tennis, skiing, playing piano, computer gaming.

Arrange informational interviews. An informational interview is a wonderful way to gain insight into jobs in your career field. First, ask a career counselor for the names of people who have the types of jobs that are of interest to you. Then, contact these people, and ask to talk with them for a short while about the nature of their job. People usually enjoy talking about their careers, especially if you are seeking information rather than explicitly asking them for a job. Talk to a counselor at the Career Services Office for advice on making the most of informational interviews.

Start networking. During college, you should begin practicing the important skill of networking, or the art of making connections with others. Networking with professionals in different careers—whether through internships you've had, informational interviews you've conducted, or alumni you've reached out to—not only will help you learn more but could also give you an advantage if jobs become available. People in your network will often remember your interest in a career field or position and want to be helpful. They might tell you about an available job opening or put in a good word if you've already applied. Networking really can open up doors.

Dealing with the Unexpected

Searching for a job is never easy and is often stressful, especially when the economy is bad. If you graduate from college at a time when jobs are scarce, you may have to look for jobs in areas outside your preferred career field. Finding a job may take you much longer than you had hoped.

Remember that you're never alone as you search for a job. Take full advantage of the Career Services Office and alumni resources on your college campus. Although they might not be able to speed up the job search process, they can provide you with support and advice as you face these difficulties. College counselors want to be as helpful and supportive as possible—in good times and bad.

⑤ WAYS THE CAREER SERVICES OFFICE CAN MAKE A DIFFERENCE

1. **Assisting with summer jobs and internships.**

   The Career Services Office can help you with work opportunities all throughout college, not just after college.

2. **Helping with professional and graduate school applications.**

   Experienced staff at the Career Services Office can help you throughout the application process, including preparing for the Graduate Record Exam and editing your applications.

3. **Providing self-assessment exercises.**

   Take advantage of self-assessment tools that can help you understand which career fields might be a good fit with your skills and interests.

4. **Connecting with other students interested in the same field.**

   Learning from students who share your interests can help you see things in a new light.

5. **Offering career advice and assistance after graduation.**

   After you graduate, you can continue to use your college's Career Services Office. Take advantage of this resource whenever you need to.

 CASE STUDY

Sasha explains how she explored her career interests in college.

After my first year, I wanted to know what careers were available to someone with a degree in economics and what steps I needed to take to do well as an economics major. Along the way, I learned some valuable lessons that helped me better understand my passions and goals.

1. *Take advantage of the resources on campus.* The Career Services Office is the best place on campus to help you figure out what you want to do with your life and how to accomplish your career goals. The office is staffed by professionals who are trained to assist college students with career-related issues. It's also a good place to meet other students who share your concerns.

2. *Meet with your advisor regularly.* I met with my advisor once a month to discuss my academic interests as well as my future interests. Advisors are there to lend a hand throughout your college career. They are familiar with the vast resources on campus and can guide you in the right direction. Be candid and honest with your advisor, even if you're not sure what career you want to pursue, so that he or she can figure out what your needs are.

3. *Join clubs that interest you.* While I was in college, I joined several organizations, such as the Black Student Union, the Business Club, and the Journal Club. I met upperclassmen who majored in economics and could help guide me in the right direction. Not only was I able to share my thoughts openly and comfortably, but I also built great relationships.

4. *Try to secure a summer internship in the fall or early spring.* It is important to start looking into summer internships as early as you can. Your internship does not need to be a paid position, but it should relate to your interests.

5. *Network on and off campus.* Networking involves much more than handing out résumés or business cards and asking for jobs or leads. To be effective at networking, you must show a genuine interest in the other person, build a strong rapport by being friendly and enthusiastic, and recognize

that networking is a two-way process in which you share information and advice.

6. *Seek out programs that can help you with internships and career development.* Most of these programs can be found at the Career Services Office. In my first year, I applied for the INROADS program, which is a rigorous career-development program designed for students with an interest in fields such as business, finance, IT, communications, and human resources.

I used a number of resources to help me explore my career interests. My summer internships were the most helpful. After my first year in college, I knew that I had an interest in finance, but I didn't know exactly what I wanted to do in that field. My internships helped shape my interest and passion. I kept a journal about my experiences; I shared my experiences and constantly sought advice.

QUESTIONS FOR REFLECTION: Have you visited the Career Services Office on your campus? If so, what have you found to be most valuable, and why? If not, consider making an appointment to learn about the extensive resources available and talking with a counselor about your interests, passions, and goals.

It's Your Life

College is a time for academic and personal exploration and growth. When you graduate, you will not be the same person you were when you entered as a first-year student. The opportunities that present themselves throughout college will help shape you. Although you won't be able to do everything at the same time, especially as you work on finding a balance in college, figure out what opportunities you don't want to miss, and make sure to build them into your overall college plan.

> ### ✓ CHECKLIST OF COLLEGE OPPORTUNITIES TO CONSIDER
>
> ☐ Volunteer opportunities that could be particularly meaningful
>
> ☐ Research experiences on or off campus
>
> ☐ Studying abroad for a term or a year
>
> ☐ Attending guest lectures or conferences about exciting topics
>
> ☐ Leading a campus organization you're passionate about

Notice What Matters to You

By embracing all that college has to offer and by noticing what you find most interesting, you'll be on your way to better understanding who you are and what you want for your future. There is so much to learn in college, and your greatest insights will sometimes come from the most unexpected places. For example, you may volunteer regularly and soon realize that you want a career that connects in some way to the cause you're so passionate about. Or studying abroad may open your eyes to global possibilities and may lead you to consider jobs in foreign countries.

You will be very busy in college, but try to pause periodically to take in all that you're experiencing and all that you're learning. Self-reflection will help you make the most of college and will allow you to consider what's really important to you. Also, remember the value of talking with and learning from others. When you reach out to others—whether it's for coffee with a mentor or for extra help in a class—you will gain a wealth of knowledge, support, and insight. Reach out, make connections, and be true to yourself. College is a time to get to know yourself. Make the most of it!

Appendix A
Living on Campus

It can be exciting to move away from home and live on campus. It may also feel overwhelming and scary. Your experience will likely include sharing space with a roommate, interacting with a residential advisor, and using relevant campus resources. To help you manage your new college life on campus, use the strategies, supports, and resources described in this appendix.

Living with Roommates

Whether you choose to live in a dorm, in an apartment on or near campus, or in a fraternity or sorority house, you'll likely live with roommates. It may be the first time you're sharing space with others, which can be a lot of fun, annoying at times, and outright difficult. In your first year, you might be able to pick your roommate. It's more likely, though, that you won't know who you'll be living with, so it's helpful to have an open mind and start from a place of mutual respect.

Mutual Respect

Mutual respect should be the basis of your relationship with your roommate (or roommates). The two (or even three, four, or more) of you will probably be sleeping, studying, and hanging out in closer quarters than you've experienced before. You may have one room stuffed with beds, desks, dressers, and closets, with barely enough room to stand. Maybe you luck out and have additional space—a bigger room or multiple rooms in a suite. Whatever your living situation, you and your roommate will need to make many adjustments as you get to know each other and learn each other's habits. You might find certain differences right away, such as race, ethnicity, or religion. And others that might arise over time—preferred bedtime, noise level, social activity, study schedule, food preferences, hygiene, or cleanliness. It's a lot to deal with. You might become fast friends with your roommate(s), or you might pass in the night with little interaction. Whatever the case, you'll have to communicate with your roommate if you want to develop the mutual respect that is necessary when living with another person.

Roommate Meetings

Hold regular roommate meetings, especially during your first weeks on campus. Discuss your preferences and figure out where you'll each have to compromise. If your roommate goes to bed several hours before you do, try to keep the noise to a minimum when he or she is asleep, or go somewhere else to socialize or study once he or she is in bed. And alternatively, if you're not an early bird, ask your roommate to turn off his or her alarm right away each morning—without hitting the snooze button a million times—and to get ready quietly while you're still in bed. There are many, many things to discuss with your roommates and issues can arise over time, even if you're communicating well.

Resolving Conflicts

It's totally normal to run into roommate conflicts. You might be familiar with fights between brothers and sisters living under the same roof. But now in college, you could be living with a stranger, so conflicts are more complicated since you're still getting to know each other. Try hard to express your concerns when you have them, and ask your roommate to do the same. The more open and respectful you can be with each other, the better living conditions you'll create together. You may decide not to live with each other after your first year, but at least you will know that you made the best of the situation and didn't sacrifice your first year embroiled in unnecessary roommate conflicts that could have been resolved.

Your Residential Advisor

Depending on your on-campus living situation, you will likely have a Residential Advisor (RA) who lives in your dorm or housing complex and is in charge of what happens on your floor or in the entire building. An RA might be an upperclassman who applied for the position or a college staff member. Your RA is an advisor, so be sure to use him or her whenever you need to.

Roommate Mediation

If you're unable to resolve roommate conflicts without assistance, call on your RA to mediate and to offer advice on how to handle them. For example, if you've agreed on room rules and don't think your roommate is abiding by them, even after you've asked nicely and made compromises, talk to your RA about what to do. You might want the RA to sit in on a few of your roommate meetings to help you establish clear ways of living together comfortably. Improving a difficult relationship is not always easy, and some roommate situations can't be resolved no matter how hard you try. If you feel that a more serious intervention is required, ask your RA whether you should talk with other resources on campus or whether you can move to a different dorm or room.

Academic and Personal Advice

Your RA can serve as a resource for other aspects of college life, including academics. In fact, at some colleges, your RA may also be your first-year academic advisor. Remember to talk to your RA if you think he or she can help you deal with academic struggles. At the very least, an RA will be able to direct you to other essential campus resources, such as the Academic Advising Office. If your RA is an upperclassman, he or she will likely have advice about certain classes that could be useful when you put together your academic plan.

If you're dealing with personal struggles, such as homesickness or anxiety, reach out to your RA and find out if he or she can help. Your RA can direct you to campus supports such as the counseling center or health center, and to make your visit easier, your RA might even be able to connect you with a specific person in the appropriate office.

Social Life

In addition to being an advisor, your RA will likely have disciplinary responsibilities concerning safety, drinking, and drugs. Even though you may develop a trusting relationship with your RA, be aware that it is the RA's job to report any inappropriate or illegal behavior to college officials, campus police, or town or city police and that you could face minor or serious consequences, depending on the behavior. Also, if you're struggling with your social life—for example, if you're feeling pressure to drink or are feeling disconnected in some way—your RA may suggest ways for you to have more fun and to take relaxing breaks.

Campus Resources

Your campus will likely have a Student Services Center with various offices, including those dedicated to living on campus. Learn about the services the center offers, and get to know staff members who can help you as questions come up.

Housing Office

If you encounter problems with facilities in your dorm or house, staff at the Housing Office should be able to assist you. The Housing Office will likely determine your housing throughout college. Although you may not be able to choose your housing in your first year, you will probably have some choice in subsequent years. On most campuses, the Housing Office administers a lottery system in which upperclassmen are randomly given a lottery number and then students choose the housing they prefer as their number comes up. If you're planning to room with others in a block, the student with the best lottery number will be the one who officially chooses housing for the group. Be sure you understand your housing options and the campus's housing rules so that you're fully aware of the process and will get the housing you need.

Dining Services

If you're living on campus, be sure you know your dining options. All campuses offer different food options and meal plans, so figure out what is best for you. If you sign up for the full meal plan, you can usually eat three times a day, seven days a week. Your meal plan might include dining halls, food courts, library cafés, and more. If you decide you won't need a full meal plan, understand what restrictions you will have—you want to be sure you will get enough to eat throughout the week.

Parking Office

Some colleges allow first-year residential students to bring cars to campus, and others don't. If you are allowed to bring your car, visit the Parking Office to understand your parking options. Sometimes having a car on campus is easy, and other times it can be more of a burden, especially if parking is scarce or if keeping your car in a lot or garage is expensive. Weigh the pros and cons of this option so that you can make a decision that is right for you.

Appendix B
Living off Campus

Attending college while living off campus is becoming more and more common. Although living off campus has many advantages, it also carries some challenges. Some students commute while balancing academics with a family. Other students are attending college after time away from school or are pursuing another degree after many years in the workforce. Whatever your situation, a variety of campus services can assist you, and you can take a number of actions to feel a connection to campus.

Find a Balance

Going to school while managing other obligations, such as a job, raising children, or caring for elderly family members, isn't easy. You face multiple demands on your time, and life is generally less predictable, making it more difficult to focus on your classes. Acknowledging the balancing act you're dealing with and potential difficulties that might arise is important as you work to also fulfill your academic responsibilities.

Nontraditional Students

If you are back in the classroom after a break of one or many years, you might feel out of place and uncomfortable, especially if your classes include younger students right out of high school. Compared with younger classmates, you have greater life experiences and more extensive responsibilities. If you're returning to college after time away or are a veteran, possibly just back from a tour of duty, your past will certainly influence your present. You might have difficulty connecting to others on campus who have not experienced what you have, making you feel stressed and lonely.

While attending college, you might also be holding down a full-time or part-time job—a juggling act that makes your schedule more complicated and increases your stress level. Sleep might be the first thing to go as you manage your college, home, and work life, and you probably have very little time for yourself. It's one thing to make it to class on time, and quite another to find time to complete assignments and study for tests as you cope with your many other demands.

Aim for a Balance

The constant juggling of your on-campus and off-campus life can take a toll, so consider what you can do to find a balance. Perhaps you can take some classes that are not killers or classes in a subject that you're already familiar with. You might decide to take fewer credits per term or to attend school part-time—you'll graduate later, but if you can keep some sanity along the way, you will likely perform better in your classes.

Consider what you can do in your off-campus life to help with the juggling act. Can you talk to your boss about working fewer hours while you work toward a degree? Can you move to a project that's less time-consuming? Can you shift your hours or sometimes work from home to make your day more manageable, especially if you have a long commute to school? If you are caring for children or elderly parents, can other family members babysit or help out during your most intense academic times (for example, when projects are due or during exams)? Do you need to let go of other obligations, such as volunteering commitments or children's activities? These are tough choices, but even small tweaks in your daily routine can save you time and energy—and might even allow you to sleep more.

Find Support

Recognize that you're not alone when you are trying to find a balance in your life. Colleges often have support services for nontraditional students or students who are veterans. Find out whether your school has a Nontraditional Student Services Office or a Veteran Student Services Office, or whether the Student Support Center has counselors dedicated to the needs of nontraditional students. Use these supports whenever you find it helpful. Making a personal connection with professional staff members on campus can help you feel more comfortable, and they can provide advice about how to deal with the many stresses you are facing.

Be honest with your advisor about your life off campus and what that will mean for you in terms of time for classes and time available to dedicate to class assignments. Your advisor can work with you to put together an academic plan that fits more easily into your daily life. Your advisor might also help you determine how to complete academic work while you're on campus, either before or after class, to maximize your time focused on classwork, away from your other obligations. Talk about this with your advisor to see what's possible.

And finally, be honest with your instructors. Introduce yourself on the first day of class. Tell them if you're returning to school after a break in your education, and ask if they might be able to support you in some way. Recognize that instructors generally want to be helpful, but they can only do that if they understand your situation.

Build a Connection

In addition to making connections with your advisor and support services staff on campus, you can also build deeper connections to the campus community and to classmates. You may not want or be able to do this, but here are some thoughts, just in case.

Join a Club or Participate in an Activity

Colleges host many different clubs and organizations. If you have a strong interest in something—music, dance, environmental concerns—or want to connect to people who share your race, ethnicity, culture, religion, or sexual orientation—consider joining a club or participate in an activity centered on these areas. You might even find an organization that brings together nontraditional students. Meeting others in the same boat is an ideal way to share stories, feel supported, get advice, and come together for fun activities.

Form a Study Group

You can connect to other students on campus through academics as well. One way to do this is by forming an in-person or online study group. The study group might convene regularly to discuss lectures, readings, and assignments, or it might convene to study for a quiz or an exam. You'll need to find ways to fit the study group into your very busy schedule—a few possibilities are communicating with your study group online or meeting during mealtimes or over the weekends.

Campus Resources

In addition to campus student services focused on the needs of nontraditional students, you should be aware of other campus resources.

Commuting

Depending on how you commute to campus, look for on-campus resources that can assist you. If you need to park a car, talk to a staff member at the campus Parking Office to find out if any parking lots or garages are available close to your classes. If you have to pay for parking, ask whether any student discounts are available. The Parking Office might also have information about car pools.

Similarly, ask if you can get a discount on bus, train, or subway passes. Your college might even run free shuttle buses to and from various locations throughout campus and your town or city. Look up the shuttle route and schedule online to find out if the shuttle is convenient for you.

Student Discounts

Besides discounts on transportation, many campuses offer student discounts on other services and activities. Check if local restaurants, movie theaters, museums, or shows offer discounted rates to students. Local bookstores or clothing stores might also offer discounts if you show your student ID.

Being a student with many other obligations off campus is challenging, but you can make connections on campus and take advantage of services if you know they exist. Seek these out to make the most of your college experience.

Acknowledgements

TEXT CREDITS

CHAPTER 3
 p. 38: Excerpted from *The American Promise: A History of the United States*, 5th ed, by James L. Roark et al. Copyright © 2012 by Bedford/St. Martin's. Used by permission of the publisher.
 p. 32: Link to VARK Questionnaire Online, Version 7.1: http://www.vark-learn.com. Copyright © Neil D. Fleming, Christchurch, New Zealand. Used by permission of VARK-Learn.com.

CHAPTER 6
 p. 81: Excerpted from *The American Promise: A History of the United States*, 5th ed, by James L. Roark et al. Copyright © 2012 by Bedford/St. Martin's. Used by permission of the publisher.

PHOTO CREDITS

CHAPTER 1
 p.1: © Cagri Oner/istockphoto; **p.6:** © Andrew Toos/CartoonStock.com; **p.12:** University of Massachusetts, Amherst

CHAPTER 2
 p.17: © Cagri Oner/istockphoto; **p.19:** © Mike Baldwin/CartoonStock.com

CHAPTER 3
 p.31: © Cagri Oner/istockphoto; **p. 34:** © 2009 Linda M. Farley; **p. 38:** From *The American Promise: A History of the United States*, 5th ed, by James L. Roark et al. Copyright © 2012 by Bedford/St. Martin's. Used by permission of the publisher.

CHAPTER 4
 p.48: © Cagri Oner/istockphoto; **p. 51:** © Loren Fishman/CartoonStock.com

CHAPTER 5
 p. 61: © Cagri Oner/istockphoto; **p. 67:** © Ralph Hagen/CartoonStock.com

CHAPTER 6
 p. 75: © Cagri Oner/istockphoto; **p. 77:** © Gary Cook/CartoonStock.com

CHAPTER 7
 p. 85: © Cagri Oner/istockphoto; **p. 88:** © Ralph Hagen/CartoonStock.com

CHAPTER 8
 p. 97: © Cagri Oner/istockphoto; **p.108:** © Jason Love/CartoonStock.com

CHAPTER 9
  p. 111: © Cagri Oner/istockphoto; **p. 122** © Grizelda/
CartoonStock.com; **p. 126:** University of Texas, Austin

CHAPTER 10
  p. 128: © Cagri Oner/istockphoto; **p. 139:** © Roy Delgado/
CartoonStock.com

CHAPTER 11
  p. 144: © Cagri Oner/istockphoto; **p.146:** U.S. Department of
Agriculture; **p. 151:** © Grizelda/CartoonStock.com

CHAPTER 12
  p. 155: © Cagri Oner/istockphoto; **p. 159:** © Ron Morgan/
CartoonStock.com; **p. 160:** Virginia Tech

CHAPTER 13
  p. 166: © Cagri Oner/istockphoto; **p. 176:** Facebook; **p. 179:**
© John McPherson/CartoonStock.com

CHAPTER 14
  p. 181: © Cagri Oner/istockphoto; **p. 190:** © Marty Bucella/
CartoonStock.com

CHAPTER 15
  p. 194: © Cagri Oner/istockphoto; **p. 200:** © Fran/
CartoonStock.com

Index

Notes

<u>**Notes**</u>

<u>**Notes**</u>

✓ CHECKLISTS

Visual Walkthroughs

QUICK TIPS

⑤ "5 THINGS" LISTS

CASE STUDIES

Contents